GOVERNMENT PROCEDURES AND OPERATIONS

WHISTLEBLOWING BY FEDERAL EMPLOYEES

BARRIERS AND PROTECTIONS

GOVERNMENT PROCEDURES AND OPERATIONS

Additional books in this series can be found on Nova's website under the Series tab.

Additional E-books in this series can be found on Nova's website under the E-book tab.

GOVERNMENT PROCEDURES AND OPERATIONS

WHISTLEBLOWING BY FEDERAL EMPLOYEES

BARRIERS AND PROTECTIONS

BERNARD L. GALLAGHER
EDITOR

nova publishers
New York

For permission to use material from this book please contact us:
Telephone 631-231-7269; Fax 631-231-8175
Web Site: http://www.novapublishers.com

Library of Congress Cataloging-in-Publication Data

ISBN: 978-1-63117-480-3

Published by Nova Science Publishers, Inc. † New York

CONTENTS

PREFACE

Chapter 1 – For more than three decades, the law has recognized the importance of encouraging Federal employees to come forward with reports of any violation of any law, rule, or regulation, or gross mismanagement, a gross waste of funds, an abuse of authority, or a substantial and specific danger to public health or safety. This report explores the extent to which Federal employees perceive wrongdoing, the extent to which they report the wrongdoing they see, and what factors influence their decisions to remain silent or to blow the whistle.

Chapter 2 – There are certain personnel practices that are, by statute, forbidden in the Federal Government. They are known as the Prohibited Personnel Practices (PPPs). One of the most frequently discussed PPPs is the prohibition against retaliating against an employee for the act of disclosing a violation of any law, rule, or regulation; gross mismanagement; a gross waste of funds; an abuse of authority; or a substantial and specific danger to public health or safety. In common parlance, such an employee is known as a whistleblower and acting against the employee because of the whistleblowing is whistleblower retaliation. However, the law can be quite different from common parlance. In the Federal Government, not everyone who discloses wrongdoing will be considered a whistleblower, and not every act of retaliation against a whistleblower is legally redressable.

Chapter 3 – This is the Public Law 112-199 (Whistleblower Protection Enhancement Act of 2012).

In: Whistleblowing by Federal Employees
Editor: Bernard L. Gallagher
ISBN: 978-1-63117-480-3

Chapter 1

BLOWING THE WHISTLE: BARRIERS TO FEDERAL EMPLOYEES MAKING DISCLOSURES*

U.S. Merit Systems Protection Board

The President
President of the Senate
Speaker of the House of Representatives

Dear Sirs:

In accordance with the requirements of 5 U.S.C. § 1204(a)(3), it is my honor to submit this U.S. Merit Systems Protection Board (MSPB) report, *Blowing the Whistle: Barriers to Federal Employees Making Disclosures*. This report discusses results from MSPB's 2010 Merit Principles Survey regarding perceptions related to whistleblowing and provides a comparison to the results of a similar survey our agency conducted in 1992.

Data from our surveys indicate that since 1992, the percentage of employees who perceive any wrongdoing has decreased. However, perceptions of retaliation against those who blow the whistle remain a serious concern. In both 1992 and 2010, approximately one-third of the individuals

* This is an edited, reformatted and augmented version of a report to the President and Congress from the U.S. Merit Systems Protection Board, dated Novmber 2011.

who felt they had been identified as a source of a report of wrongdoing also perceived either threats or acts of reprisal, or both. Additionally, training for employees about the protections available to whistleblowers has improved since 1992, but given that such training is mandated by law, there are still far too many employees who have not received this information.

The survey data also indicate that the most important factor for employees when deciding whether to report wrongdoing is not the personal consequences for the employee. Saving lives was more important to survey respondents than whether they would experience punishment or a reward, and whether the agency would act on a report of wrongdoing mattered more than any fear of an unpleasant consequence for the employee making the report. This means that agencies have the power to influence employees' decisions about reporting wrongdoing. The most important step that agencies can take to prevent wrongdoing may be the creation of a culture that supports whistleblowing.

I believe you will find this report useful as you consider issues affecting the Federal Government's ability to operate efficiently and effectively in these challenging times.

Respectfully,

Susan Tsui Grundmann

U.S. MERIT SYSTEMS PROTECTION BOARD

The U.S. Merit Systems Protection Board ("MSPB" or "The Board") is an independent, quasi-judicial agency in the Executive branch that serves as the guardian of Federal merit systems. The Board was established by the Civil Service Reform Act of 1978 (CSRA), Public Law No. 95-454.

The Board's mission is to protect Federal merit systems and the rights of individuals within those systems. MSPB carries out its statutory responsibilities and authorities primarily by adjudicating individual employee appeals and by conducting merit systems studies.

The topic of this report, whistleblowing, occurs at the intersection of MSPB's two missions. As a part of its adjudicatory mission, MSPB considers, among other types of cases, appeals brought by individuals who allege that they have been subjected to retaliatory personnel actions because they have disclosed a violation of any law, rule, or regulation, or gross mismanagement, a gross waste of funds, an abuse of authority, or a substantial and specific danger to public health or safety.

As a part of the studies mission, MSPB has the statutory responsibility to study the health of the merit systems and the extent to which the public's interest in a civil service free from prohibited personnel practices is being protected. An efficient and effective civil service—a merit principle—requires a workplace in which employees feel that they can safely blow the whistle on wrongdoing. This report is issued solely under the studies function of the MSPB, and any findings or recommendations are not an official "opinion" of the Board in its adjudicatory role.

EXECUTIVE SUMMARY

For more than three decades, the law has recognized the importance of encouraging Federal employees to come forward with reports of any violation of any law, rule, or regulation, or gross mismanagement, a gross waste of funds, an abuse of authority, or a substantial and specific danger to public health or safety.[1] This report explores the extent to which Federal employees perceive wrongdoing, the extent to which they report the wrongdoing they see, and what factors influence their decisions to remain silent or to blow the whistle.

Findings and Recommendations

Survey data show that since 1992, the percentage of employees who perceive any wrongdoing has decreased.[2] However, perceptions of retaliation against those who blow the whistle remain a serious concern. In both 1992 and 2010, approximately one-third of the individuals who felt they had been identified as a source of a report of wrongdoing also perceived either threats or acts of reprisal, or both. One possible cause for this level of perception may be differences between how the law defines whistleblowing for purposes of protecting individuals from retaliation and how employees define it.[3]

The survey data also indicate that the most important factors for employees when deciding whether to report wrongdoing are not about the personal consequences for the employee. Saving lives is more important to respondents than whether they will experience punishment or a reward, and whether the agency will act on a report of wrongdoing matters more than any fear of an unpleasant consequence for the employee making the report.

This means that agencies have the power to influence employees' decisions about reporting wrongdoing. We urge agencies to create cultures in which employees will believe that:

- Supervisors and managers want to be told about wrongdoing;
- Supervisors and managers want their employees to come forward to report any basis for a reasonable suspicion of wrongdoing without requiring absolute proof of wrongdoing;
- A report of wrongdoing will result in positive changes; and
- An employee will not be shunned or punished for reporting wrongdoing, but instead will be supported or praised.

Survey data also show that agencies are doing more to train employees about whistleblower protection rights. However, given that this training is mandated by law, there are still far too many employees who reported that they did not receive this training. We therefore urge agencies to improve the quality of employee training about how to make a disclosure, an employee's right to not experience retaliation or threats of retaliation, and how employees can exercise that right.

Our data show that perceptions of retaliation among those identified as the source of a report of wrongdoing have not declined since 1992. As noted in our recent report, *Whistleblower Protections for Federal Employees*, the laws to protect whistleblowers are complex and can create challenging situations for employees. It is possible that amending the law regarding the circumstances under which an individual is eligible for protection as a whistleblower may be beneficial. We encourage Congress to continue to examine and debate how best to achieve the delicate balance between effective management control of the workplace and the need to ensure that employees can bring wrongdoing to light without fear of threatened or actual retaliation.

INTRODUCTION

In the Civil Service Reform Act of 1978 (CSRA), Congress made it illegal to use a personnel action to retaliate against an employee (or applicant for employment) because of the individual's disclosure of a violation of any law, rule, or regulation, or gross mismanagement, a gross waste of funds, an abuse of authority, or a substantial and specific danger to public health or safety.[4] The law to protect whistleblowers was strengthened by the Whistleblower Protection Act of 1989 and its 1994 amendments. The law is remedial—it provides some redress for retaliation. However, to achieve the purpose of the law—encouraging employees to make disclosures—the Government must do more than just provide legal protections against retaliation. Individual agencies must also create cultures that persuade employees that their whistleblowing will make a positive difference towards preventing wrongdoing.

Purpose

The U.S. Merit Systems Protection Board fulfills its mission in part by conducting studies related to the civil service and other merit systems.[5] It is a merit system principle that all employees should maintain high standards of integrity, conduct, and concern for the public interest.[6] Disclosing wrongdoing is an important aspect of this principle. MSPB recently issued a report on how the law does and does not protect individuals from reprisal for whistleblowing activities.[7] To complete the picture, this report will look at the extent to which employees feel able to make these disclosures, and what can be done to encourage more disclosures in the future.

Survey Methodology

This report relies upon data from MSPB's Merit Principles Surveys (MPSs) conducted in 1992 and 2010. In 1992, the survey was administered to 20,851 employees, with 13,432 respondents (representing a 64 percent response rate). The results were published in *Whistleblowing in the Federal Government: An Update*, available at www.mspb.gov/studies.

The 2010 MPS was administered to 71,970 Federal employees in the departments and agencies listed below.[8] We oversampled certain populations to ensure a sufficient amount of responses from some subagencies. The final results have therefore been weighted to ensure that the outcomes are representative of most of the Federal Government as a whole.

Survey participation was voluntary. There was a 58 percent response rate overall. Participating departments and agencies included:

- Department of the Air Force
- Department of the Army
- Department of the Navy
- Department of Defense (Other)
- Department of Agriculture
- Department of Commerce
- Department of Justice
- Department of Labor
- Department of Energy
- Department of Education
- Department of Health and Human Services
- Department of Homeland Security
- Department of Housing and Urban Development
- Department of Interior
- Department of State
- Department of Transportation
- Department of the Treasury
- Department of Veterans Affairs
- Environmental Protection Agency
- Federal Deposit Insurance Corporation
- General Services Administration
- National Aeronautics and Space Administration
- Office of Personnel Management
- Social Security Administration

We also sent a brief questionnaire to 32 agencies' Offices of the Inspectors General (OIGs). Twenty-four OIGs responded.

Wrongdoing, Whistleblowing, and Retaliation over Time

The percentage of respondents who have perceived wrongdoing in their agency has decreased since 1992. Furthermore, respondents are: (1) slightly more likely to report the wrongdoing; (2) less likely to be identified as the source of the report; and (3) less likely to perceive a negative consequence for making the report. However, of those who made a report and were identified as the source, the percentage of respondents who personally experienced reprisal or a threat of reprisal remains virtually unchanged.[9]

When looking at this data, it is important to—as always—caution our audience against reading too much into small changes in survey results. First of all, our MPS is a survey of perceptions, which are subject to human error. An event can occur without being perceived, or can be inaccurately perceived. Additionally, as the size of a sample population shrinks, the margin for error grows.[10] Our questions began with a survey sample of more than 40,000 respondents for 2010, and over 13,000 respondents for 1992. However, with each level of drilling down into respondents who provided a particular answer to a prior question, the population answering the next question becomes much smaller.[11] Furthermore, in this report, we are comparing only two points in time. As can be seen in our recent report, *Prohibited Personnel Practices: Employee Perceptions*, available at www. mspb.gov/studies, data regarding perceptions can fluctuate over time and trends do not always occur in a straight line.

Wrongdoing

Whistleblower protection laws and policies exist to encourage employees to come forward with information they may have about wrongdoing so that the wrongdoing can be addressed and prevented in the future. However, as explained in our recent report, *Whistleblower Protections for Federal Employees*, not all forms of wrongdoing are protected by the law. It is therefore possible for an employee to perceive that he or she has reported someone doing something "wrong" while the law does not consider the report a protected act of whistleblowing. In order to qualify for protection under the Whistleblower Protection Act, the individual must be disclosing a violation of a law, rule, or regulation; gross mismanagement; a gross waste of funds; an abuse of authority; or a substantial and specific danger to public health or safety.[12] Because each of these terms has its own definition, it is not practical to educate respondents in a survey as to what "wrongdoing" means under the law. As a result, our respondents were instructed that for purposes of the survey, the term "wrongdoing" refers to the creation or tolerance in the workplace of a health or safety danger, unlawful behavior, fraud, waste, or abuse. Some of our questions used the term wrongdoing, while others used a more specific description of the conduct at issue.

For example, our 1992 and 2010 surveys inquired: "During the last 12 months, did you personally observe or obtain direct evidence of one or more illegal or wasteful activities involving your agency?" In 1992, 17.7 percent of respondents answered yes, and 82.3 percent answered no. In 2010, only 11.1 percent of respondents answered yes, and 88.9 percent answered no. This data indicates that perceptions that wrongdoing has occurred have dropped by more than a third between 1992 and 2010.

However, as can be seen in table 1, below, the nature of the wrongdoing that was perceived has changed only slightly since 1992, with fewer perceptions of waste caused by unnecessary or deficient goods or services, and more waste perceived in the area of badly managed programs. This may be a result of a shift in the Government to a more knowledge-based workforce. With more employees managing and analyzing programs, there may simply be more opportunities to observe wrongdoing in this arena. Declines in perceptions of waste caused by unnecessary or deficient goods or services may be a result of the attention paid in recent years to the need for better contracting controls and improvements in the way contracting officers and their technical representatives are selected and trained.[13] However, all of the differences between 1992 and 2010 on the table below are within the margin for error, and may not be indicative of major changes in perceptions about how often various types of wrongdoing occur in Federal agencies.

Table 1. Percentage of respondents indicating that the most serious wrongdoing they observed in the last 12 months was in a particular category

1992	2010	Categories
1.9%	1.8%	Stealing Federal funds
6.3%	3.1%	Stealing Federal property
0.2%	0.2%	Accepting bribes or kickbacks
5.0%	5.1%	Waste caused by ineligible people receiving funds, goods, or services
17.9%	13.8%	Waste caused by unnecessary or deficient goods or services
11.9%	10.1%	Use of an official position for personal benefit
35.3%	38.9%	Waste caused by a badly managed program
3.9%	4.8%	Unfair advantage in the selection of a contractor, consultant, or vendor
4.8%	4.6%	Tolerating a situation or practice which poses a substantial and specific danger to public health or safety
13.0%	17.6%	Other serious violation of law or regulation

When asked where the activity occurred, the greatest difference between the 1992 and 2010 responses was the decrease in perceptions that wrongdoing was occurring outside the workgroup but within the agency—nearly 15 percentage points. However, as can be seen in table 2, below, there was not a corresponding drop in perceptions inside the workgroup. Further research would be necessary to determine why these perceptions about the location of wrongdoing have changed.

Table 2. Percentage of respondents indicating that wrongdoing occurred in a particular location*

1992	2010	
43.8%	48.5%	Your workgroup
64.2%	49.4%	Outside your workgroup, but within your agency
5.4%	3.3%	Another Federal agency
12.2%	8.1%	Contractor or vendor
2.4%	4.5%	Other

* Respondents were instructed to select all that applied.

The purpose of whistleblower protection laws is to encourage employees to report wrongdoing so that management can make programs more efficient and effective, particularly in terms of preventing taxpayer dollars from being wasted. However, as can be seen in figure 1, below, the cost of wrongdoing has increased since 1992. This does not necessarily mean that waste or fraud consumes a larger share of government resources, but it is certainly possible. According to the bureau of labor statistics, $5,000 in 1992 equates to $7,771 in 2010. As products and labor become more expensive, it makes sense that there would be more money at stake in any wrongdoing. Respondents may also be more aware of and sensitive to the financial costs of wrongdoing in the current environment of tight budgets. Because our questions in 1992 and 2010 asked respondents to select from a range of values, and not to provide a specific dollar amount, we cannot report if, after adjusting for inflation, the real cost of the perceived wrongdoing has increased or decreased from 1992 to 2010. However, given the jump in the "more than $100,000" category from 23 percent to 35 percent, there is the possibility that after adjustment for inflation, the cost of individual acts of wrongdoing may have increased.[14]

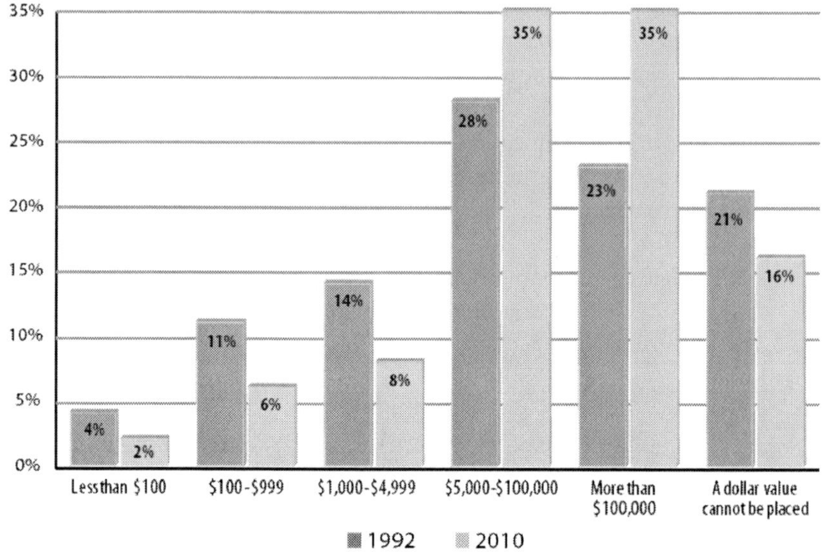

*Not adjusted for inflation.

Figure 1. Cost of Wrongdoing by Year.*

However, the news with respect to costs is not all bad. While the perceived cost ofwrongdoing went up between 1992 and 2010, the perceived frequency with which the wrongdoing occurred went down very slightly, as can be seen in table 3, below. Respondents in 2010 were more likely than respondents in 1992 to report that the wrongdoing happened once or rarely, and less likely to report that it was occasional or frequent. While the differences in data from 1992 and 2010 are relatively minor, we can, at least, report that perceptions of wrongdoing appear not to have increased in frequency.

Table 3. Percentage of respondents indicating that wrongdoing occurred with a particular level of frequency

1992	2010	Frequency
12.8%	14.1%	Once or rarely
33.0%	27.2%	Occasionally
46.0%	44.4%	Frequently
8.2%	14.3%	Don’t know/Can’t judge

Whistleblowing

While observing wrongdoing is the first step in the whistleblowing process, not everyone who sees wrongdoing chooses to tell anyone else what they have observed. To blow the whistle, someone has to make some noise. In 2010, respondents were slightly less likely to report that they did not tell anyone about the wrongdoing that they observed compared with survey data from 1992, but in both years, a strong majority of employees told someone. As can be seen in table 4, below, the percentage of respondents who told no one what they observed dropped from 40 percent in 1992 to 34 percent in 2010. In 2010, family, friends, and coworkers were less likely to be told about the wrongdoing than they were in 1992. However, this did not correspond to substantially more people reporting wrongdoing to management. Instead, it seems that venting to equally powerless people dropped, but the willingness of respondents to take action that could lead to change was not substantially changed.[15] (Our next chapter discusses what motivates employees to decide to act and blow the whistle.)

Table 4. Percentage of respondents indicating that they reported the observed activity to a particular individual

1992	2010	
39.8%	35.0%	I did not report the activity
26.6%	20.5%	Family member or friend
37.1%	35.9%	Co-worker
35.9%	33.4%	Immediate supervisor
20.2%	19.9%	Higher level supervisor
8.0%	8.6%	Higher level agency official
5.6%	5.1%	Agency Inspector General
0.7%	1.1%	Office of Special Counsel
0.3%	0.6%	Government Accountability Office
2.7%	1.5%	Law enforcement official
5.7%	7.2%	Union representative
0.2%	0.6%	News media
1.9%	1.8%	Congressional staff member or member of Congress
0.7%	0.6%	Advocacy group outside the Government
3.8%	8.8%	Other

* Respondents were instructed to select all that applied.

Retaliation

In order to encourage employees to blow the whistle, the law seeks to protect whistleblowers from personnel actions being threatened or taken because of an employee's disclosure of wrongdoing.[16] However, not all forms of unpleasantness take the form of personnel actions. While retaliatory personnel actions are illegal, other forms of unpleasantness are not. As we explained in our recent report, *Whistleblower Protections for Federal Employees*, a personnel action is:

1) An appointment;
2) A promotion;
3) An action under chapter 75 of Title 5 or other disciplinary or corrective action;
4) A detail, transfer, or reassignment;
5) A reinstatement;
6) A restoration;
7) A reemployment;
8) A performance evaluation under chapter 43 of Title 5;
9) A decision concerning pay, benefits, or awards, or concerning education or training if the education or training may reasonably be expected to lead to an appointment, promotion, performance evaluation, or other action described in this subparagraph;
10) A decision to order psychiatric testing or examination; or
11) Any other significant change in duties, responsibilities, or working conditions.[17]

As will be discussed in greater depth in our next chapter, the ability of whistleblowers to protect their identity is important to them. Their ability to achieve this anonymity appears to have improved since 1992, as can be seen in table 5, below. In 1992, 53 percent of respondents who made a disclosure reported that they were identified as the source. In 2010, 43 percent reported that they were identified.

The clearest reason to avoid being identified is to avoid being the target of people who are unhappy about someone making a report of wrongdoing. Our surveys asked respondents about retaliatory personnel actions as well as other forms of unpleasantness. The percentage of respondents who stated that they were identified as the source of a report of wrongdoing without experiencing any unpleasantness increased from 37 percent in 1992 to 44 percent in 2010.

As can be seen in table 6, below, of the forms of unpleasantness that were perceived, the greatest drop in perception was that someone above the respondent's supervisor was unhappy with the respondent for having reported the problem. While there is, of course, more progress to be made, this could reflect a positive trend regarding agency leadership attitudes that we hope to see continued in the future.

Table 5. Percentage of respondents indicating that they were identified as the source of the report

1992	2010	Identified
53.1%	42.5%	Yes, I was identified
46.9%	57.5%	No, I was not identified

Table 6. Percentage of respondents reporting a particular effect as a result of being identified as the source of a report of wrongdoing

1992	2010	Effect
9.2%	7.1%	I was given credit by my management for having reported the problem
37.2%	44.0%	Nothing happened to me for having reported the problem
18.4%	17.6%	My coworkers were unhappy with me for having reported the problem
31.2%	28.6%	My supervisor was unhappy with me for having reported the problem
35.8%	28.0%	Someone above my supervisor was unhappy with me for having reported the problem
12.2%	13.3%	I was threatened with reprisal for having reported the problem
18.7%	21.6%	I received an actual reprisal for having reported the problem

However, we also asked a slightly differently worded question on both surveys: Within the last 12 months, have you personally experienced some type of reprisal or threat of reprisal by management for having reported an activity? (This question did not require the respondent to consider the nature of the threatened or actual reprisal.) The answer to this question remained virtually unchanged, with 36.9 percent of respondents answering yes to this question in 1992, and 36.2 percent answering yes in 2010. Thus, the fact remains that while there may have been less wrongdoing to report in 2010, among those who made such reports, perceptions of retaliation and threats of retaliation remained a serious problem.

Some of the responses that we received from OIGs also indicated that retaliation is occurring in some cases. We asked the OIGs, "Given what you know about how the system actually works, if someone you deeply cared about privately asked you if they should make a disclosure to an OIG office, what advice would you give?" Many OIGs reported that they would encourage the disclosure, but most also included a cautionary note about the potential consequences, especially the potential for retaliation.

The consequences of retaliation are typically felt most strongly by the whistleblower, but others can be affected as well. As noted in our recent report, *Prohibited Personnel Practices: Employee Perceptions*, employees who are not personally affected by the commission of a prohibited personnel practice may notice when it happens to others in the work unit, and such perceptions can affect the observer's level of engagement. This is particularly true for the prohibited personnel practice of retaliation for whistleblowing. Thus, in addition to the chilling effect that perceptions of retaliation may have on the willingness of other employees to blow the whistle in the future, perceptions of retaliation for whistleblowing activities also harms the efficiency of the service in other ways.

Possible explanations for these perceptions of retaliation and threats of retaliation include: (1) differences in the way the law defines a protected disclosure versus what respondents consider a report of wrongdoing; (2) differences in the way the law defines retaliation versus what respondents perceive as retaliation; (3) poor communication by management as to its actual motives when discussing actions or potential actions resulting in assumptions of retaliatory causes; or (4) agencies engaging in reprisal or threats of reprisal as defined by law following employee disclosures as defined by law.

Different causes for perceptions of retaliation or threats of retaliation call for different solutions. Where a lack of education is at fault, agencies should better educate their workforces about what constitutes whistleblowing and retaliation under Federal law. (Our recent report, *Whistleblowing Protections for Federal Employees*, available at www.mspb.gov/ studies, may be helpful to any educational efforts.)

Where poor communication creates the perceptions, supervisors should be made more aware of how their decisions are perceived and the need to better communicate the reasons behind their decisions. Lastly, where agency officials are engaged in retaliation or threats of retaliation against individuals who disclose wrongdoing, agency leaders need to address the conduct of those supervisors as well as any agency culture that permits such activities to exist.

Congress has debated in recent years whether the law, as currently written, does enough to protect those who report wrongdoing. Because the Board adjudicates whistleblowing retaliation claims and must apply the law as written and as interpreted by our reviewing court, the Board has not taken a position on any proposed changes to the law. However, these debates are very important because, as explained in our recent report *Whistleblowing Protections for Federal Employees*, the laws to protect whistleblowers are complex and can create challenging situations for employees. Accordingly, we encourage Congress to continue to examine which rules and definitions it deems most appropriate to strike the delicate balance between effective management control of the workplace and the need to ensure that employees can safely bring wrongdoing to light.

As shown in table 7 below, employees currently perceive a wide variety of forms of reprisal.[18] Many types of reprisal showed dramatic increases in perception, particularly being fired, which increased more than nine fold from the percentage in 1992. This percentage of respondents indicating they experienced being fired is odd, because once an employee has been removed, the individual would not be in our survey sample unless he or she had been returned to the position, or had been given a new appointment. However, perceived denials of promotions, opportunities for training, transfers to a new location, suspensions, and demotions all more than doubled in both threats and experienced actions. We note that in 2010, approximately 400 out of more than 40,000 respondents indicated that within the last 12 months, they perceived that they had personally experienced some type of reprisal or threat of reprisal by management for having reported an activity. With a respondent group of only 400, the margin for error is +/- 5 percent. While some of these increased perceptions are within that margin for error, several are substantially outside of it.[19]

As shown in table 8, below, how respondents reacted to the perceived retaliation has changed since 1992. Most notably, employees are less likely to report that they took no action, and more likely to have exercised some avenue of redress.

One possible explanation for employees being more active in response to perceived retaliation may be improvements in the education of those employees. In our 1992 survey, we asked respondents how knowledgeable they were about the actions they could take if they were to blow the whistle and were retaliated against. In response, 67 percent said they knew "little" or "nothing." And, when we asked them in 1992 if their agencies had specifically informed them of their rights if retaliated against for whistleblowing, 79 percent said "no."[20] In contrast, in 2010, 55 percent of respondents stated that they agreed that their agency had educated them about what their rights would be if they disclosed wrongdoing, 21 percent neither agreed nor disagreed, and 24 percent disagreed.

Table 7. Percentage of respondents reporting that a reprisal or threatened reprisal took a particular form

1992		2010		Activity
Threatened	Experienced	Threatened	Experienced	
11.8%	48.2%	10.8%	50.3%	Poor performance appraisal
5.1%	18.5%	10.3%	38.9%	Denial of promotion
1.5%	19.0%	6.6%	39.8%	Denial of opportunity for training
2.6%	30.7%	8.4%	46.8%	Denial of award
8.0%	36.1%	9.3%	45.9%	Assignment to less desirable or less important duties
3.8%	22.9%	6.1%	29.1%	Transfer or reassignment to a different job with less desirable duties
3.1%	5.2%	7.1%	13.7%	Reassignment to a different geographical location
3.3%	2.5%	6.8%	14.7%	Suspension from my job
1.9%	0.7%	9.1%	8.9%	Fired from my job
3.9%	3.1%	3.6%	14.8%	Grade level demotion
3.1%	48.8%	9.1%	63.5%	Shunned by coworkers or managers
8.7%	47.6%	11.9%	54.3%	Verbal harassment or intimidation
2.0%	1.6%	1.4%	6.1%	Required to take a fitness for duty exam
5.3%	14.5%	8.0%	32.7%	Other

*Respondents were able to select both the "threatened" and "experienced" option for each item if both a threat of retaliation and the actual retaliation occurred.

While there has been clear improvement in the extent to which agencies have educated employees about their rights with regard to retaliation, more must be done. Under the No Fear Act, agencies are required by law to provide training to their employees regarding their rights and remedies under whistleblower protection laws.[21] That approximately a quarter of respondents in 2010 disagreed that they had been trained about these rights may indicate that the training has been lacking in some way.

The source of the problem may be that the training being provided is not effective, or that the training is not reaching some employees. In either case, this lack of training is unfortunate, because training appears to have a relationship to respondents' perceptions about the adequacy of the protections in place for whistleblowers. Of those employees who agreed that their agency had educated them about what their rights would be if they disclosed wrongdoing, 74 percent agreed that the protections against reprisal for disclosing wrongdoing are adequate. In contrast, when respondents reported that their agency did not educate them about their rights, only 14 percent of respondents believed there were adequate protections.

Table 8. Percentage of respondents reporting a particular response to a perceived reprisal or threat of reprisal

1992	2010	
45.2%	26.4%	Took no action
36.2%	37.6%	Complained to a higher level of agency management
8.4%	15.6%	Complained to the Office of Inspector General within agency
31.8%	29.9%	Complained to some other office within agency (for example, the Personnel Office or EEO Office)
17.3%	20.3%	Filed a complaint through union representative
12.1%	14.9%	Filed a formal grievance within agency
16.2%	23.7%	Filed an EEO (discrimination) complaint
1.9%	9.2%	Filed a complaint with the Office of Special Counsel
1.7%	4.0%	Filed an action with the Merit Systems Protection Board
11.9%	18.4%	Took an action not listed above

We encourage agencies to consider the training they are providing and the means by which it is provided to see if more effective training programs can be developed in order to increase employee education as mandated by the No Fear Act. However, while the training should be improved, the No Fear Act training that has been provided may be having some effect. As shown in table 8, above, employees' use of OSC and their particular agencies' EEO office to address retaliation appears to have increased. As the No Fear Act specifically requires agencies to educate employees about their rights with respect to discrimination and retaliation for whistleblowing, an increase in education may have played some role in the increase in the use of these two avenues for redress. We are also encouraged by respondents' increased use of their particular agency's Office of the Inspector General. It appears that progress has been made, but more can still be done.

BARRIERS AND MOTIVATORS FOR WHISTLEBLOWING

Because one of our goals is to identify what might currently serve as a barrier to whistleblowing, and what agencies can do to encourage employees to make disclosures in the future, this chapter concentrates on data from the 2010 MPS. For those questions that were asked in both 1992 and 2010, a comparison of the data can be found in the Appendix.

Additionally, unlike the last chapter which dealt with increasingly fewer respondents as we went deeper into the whistleblower retaliation process, this chapter uses questions asked of all respondents, which allows us to work with a much smaller margin for error— approximately one half of one percent.

Consequences of the Wrongdoing

In order to see what agencies could do better to encourage disclosures of wrongdoing, we asked survey respondents what would encourage them to report an illegal or wasteful activity. The potential consequences of the wrongdoing, if left unchecked, were extremely important to the respondents. Not surprisingly, as can be seen in figure 2, below, the most important consideration for respondents was whether the wrongdoing might endanger people's lives, followed by the risk of a serious cost to the Government. Personal considerations such as protection from reprisal were somewhat less likely to be important to respondents than people's lives or Government property, and the likelihood of receiving a reward carried even less weight for most respondents.

Management Reaction to the Report

Because barriers to reporting wrongdoing and the question of what can be done to encourage more reports is so important, we also approached the issue from another direction, focusing more heavily on the many different considerations that could come into play.

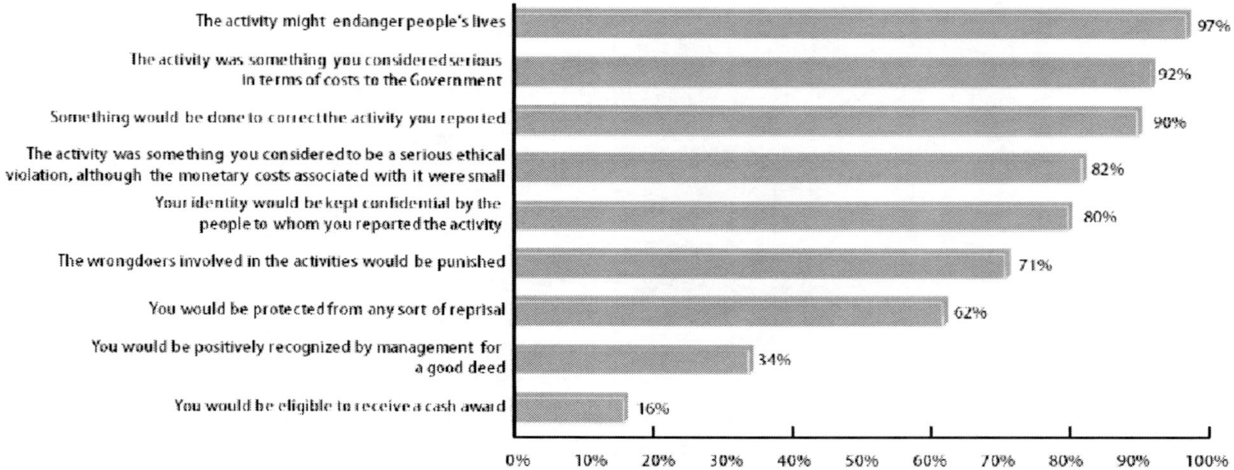

Figure 2. Percentage of respondents indicating a particular consequence would be important to their decision to report wrongdoing.

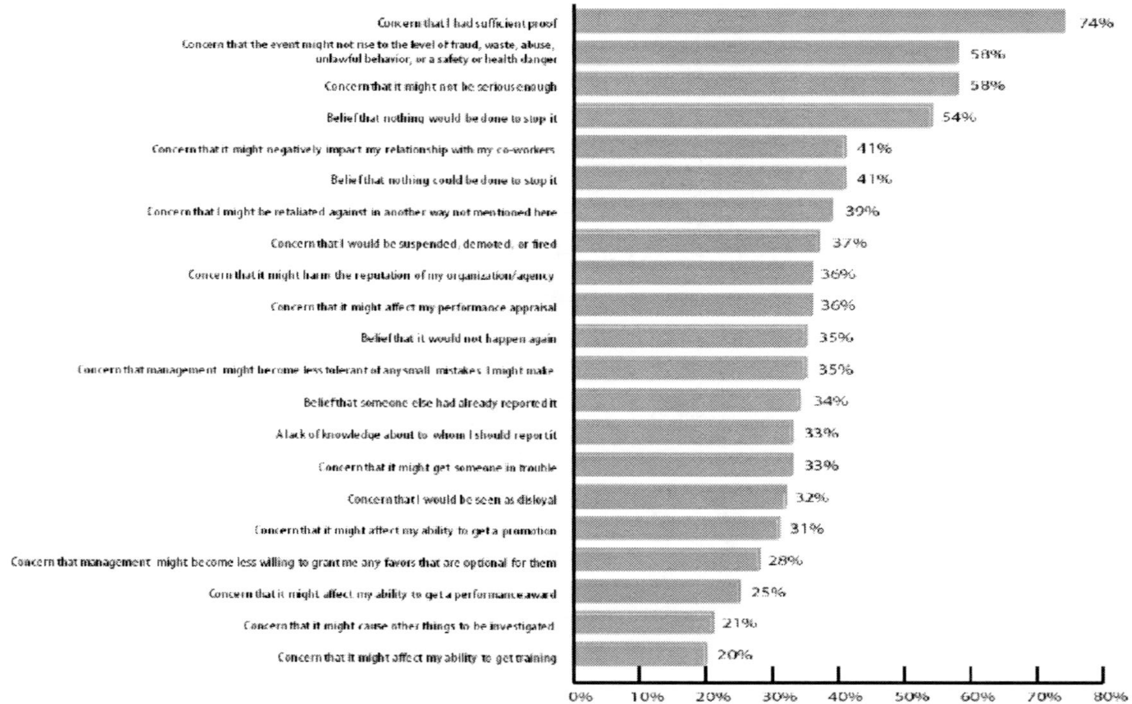

Figure 3. Percentage of respondents indicating that a particular concern would affect their decision to report wrongdoing to some or a great extent.

We asked respondents, "If tomorrow you were to observe a health or safety danger, unlawful behavior, fraud, waste, or abuse, to what extent do you think that each of the following would factor into your decision on whether or not to report the wrongdoing?" and provided a long list of possible considerations. As can be seen in figure 3 below, respondents continued to emphasize whether something would likely be done, whereas personal consequences, although important to more than a third of the workforce, were nevertheless more likely to be considered to only a little extent or not at all.

It appears that respondents want to be sure that they are right about the wrongdoing, and that if they make a report, they will be able to back it up. But, the question of whether something would be done to stop the wrongdoing, which can be closely tied to how well the individual can prove serious wrongdoing, remained high on the list for respondents.

The third most important factor on the short list (consequences, figure 2), and the fourth most important factor on the long list (concerns, figure 3), are within management's control: Will management do something if they are told about the wrongdoing? Even more than desiring self-protection, employees want to know that if they risk subjecting themselves to the negative consequences that may come with being perceived as a "tattletale" they are not taking a risk just to fail. If managers can persuade employees that making a report will make a difference, managers can greatly increase the potential that employees will give them valuable information to correct wrongdoing that has occurred and prevent it from happening again.

Agencies can also act to mitigate any negative effect from the top three concerns in figure 3: sufficiency of the proof; perceived seriousness of the wrongdoing; and concern as to whether the wrongdoing rises to the level of fraud, waste or abuse. The key to addressing these factors is for management to assure the workforce that management will not require absolute proof of wrongdoing or a particularly high level of serious consequences in order for management to care about and seriously investigate the potential wrongdoing.

The whistleblower protection laws do not require an individual to show proof that he or she was right, only that his or her conclusions were reasonable.[22] Similarly, the laws can protect a whistleblower, even if the wrongdoing being disclosed is unlikely to result in death or serious injuries. Less serious acts of wrongdoing are still wrong, and a disclosure of such acts is still subject to protection under the law if the wrongdoing is addressed in 5 U.S.C. § 2302(b)(8). While 5 U.S.C. § 2302(b)(8) addresses acts of retaliation, we encourage management to take a similar, expansive approach to deciding what to do about potential wrongdoing. Reporting of reasonable suspicions of wrongdoing should be encouraged, and "minor" wrongdoing is still wrong.

When an individual brings potential wrongdoing to management's attention, the report should be given serious consideration, and if it seems reasonable to suspect that wrongdoing may have occurred, management should look into the matter more deeply. If management is unable to consider the situation impartially, possibly due to relationships with those involved or a stake in the outcome, the matter should be referred to an impartial individual or office for consideration, such as the Inspector General.

If, after an investigation, it turns out that the individual making the report was incorrect about there being wrongdoing, management should still let the individual know: (1) that the allegation was treated seriously; (2) why management concluded that wrongdoing did not occur; and (3) that the individual did the right thing coming forward and is encouraged to do so again if he or she has a reasonable suspicion that something is improper.

If the investigation reveals that wrongdoing did occur, management should address the wrongdoing, take measures to prevent it from happening again, and let the person who reported it know (to the extent that it is permitted) what management did about the situation. Even if management cannot give the individual details about how the situation was addressed (perhaps because of privacy laws or an ongoing criminal action), management should do what it can, within those limits, to let the reporter know that action was taken and that by coming forward, the reporter made a positive contribution to the public service.

Reports of wrongdoing that do not appear to be based on a reasonable suspicion may need to be handled more delicately. As the Federal Circuit has noted, "[d]iscussion and even disagreement with supervisors over job-related activities is a normal part of most occupations."[23] Sometimes, the supervisor will have additional information that can explain why there is no cause for concern. Or, perhaps, when faced with the same information, an impartial supervisor might not think it reasonable to be suspicious. But, just because a supervisor does not share an employee's perceptions regarding potential wrongdoing in one situation does not mean that the employee will never observe wrongdoing in the future that the agency should know about. If, when making a report, the employee feels ignored or that the employee's concerns are given no value, the employee might be discouraged from coming forward in the future with important information.

Furthermore, as noted in our recent report, *Prohibited Personnel Practices: Employee Perceptions*, employees observe how others in their work unit are treated and make judgments about management from those observations.[24] If management is willing to listen fairly to one employee, others may conclude that they too can come to management with their perceptions of wrongdoing. If, on the other hand, employees see their peers being treated dismissively, they may conclude that it is unwise to bother reporting any wrongdoing they have observed themselves. This environment can deprive management of the opportunity to gather important information to protect the agency and the public.

If wrongdoing is happening, it is much better for the agency, and the public, if swift action can be taken to intercede. The American people have a right to know when wrongdoing occurs in their government. However, waiting until the problem gets more serious, or leaks out to the press, is not in the best interest of the agency. The story can be about how an agency identified a problem and fixed it, or the story can be about how an agency ignored or allowed a serious condition to go unchecked.

We recognize that the following recommendation will require a change in culture in some agencies, but we firmly believe that agencies should publicly praise their whistleblowers. Once a problem exists, ignoring it is unlikely to accomplish anything except make it worse. But, going public and saying, "We have great employees who care about preventing wrongdoing and a culture that supports them," speaks far more highly of an organization than trying to distract people from the issues by attacking the person who comes forward. Praising the whistleblower and speaking openly about how the agency reacted to the whistleblowing will also help persuade employees that reporting wrongdoing will likely result in something being done about the wrongdoing—a factor that weighs heavily with most employees. Unfortunately, when we asked our 2010 MPS respondents if they would be praised at work for disclosing wrongdoing, only 22 percent agreed that this would occur.

Current Perceptions of Agency Culture

The importance of cultural improvements was another area stressed by the OIGs. We asked the OIGs what agencies could do under the current laws to increase the potential that an employee who observes wrongdoing would report it. Several OIGs responded that it would be helpful if senior leadership sent the message to the workforce that as Federal employees, reporting wrongdoing is an important part of their jobs and a valuable public service.

As can be seen in figure 4, below, less than two-thirds of respondents agreed that their agency actively encourages employees to report wrongdoing. Additionally, only forty-two percent of respondents reported that they could disclose wrongdoing without making their lives any harder. Lastly, as mentioned earlier, when we asked respondents if they would be praised for reporting wrongdoing, only 22 percent agreed that this would happen. Thus, it is clear that more should be done to improve agency cultures.

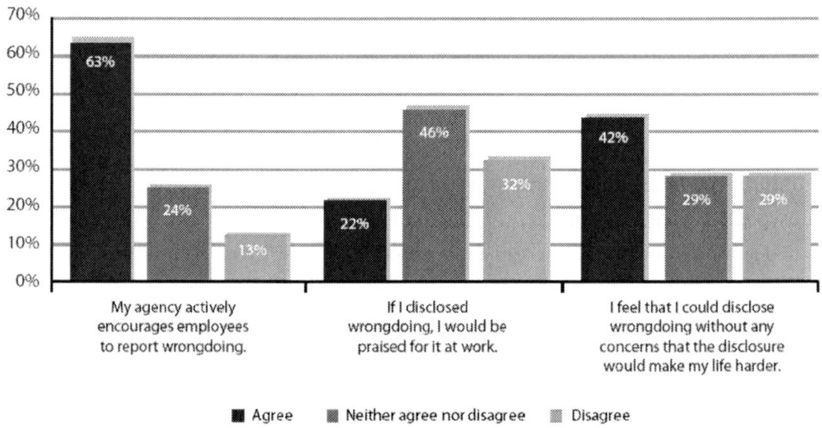

Figure 4. Percentage of respondents indicating an agency culture that supports whistleblowing.

Trust that wrongdoing can be safely exposed is important for reasons beyond the benefits of management learning important information about wrongdoing. Of those employees who reported feeling that they could disclose wrongdoing without any concerns that the disclosurewouldmake life harder, 64.7 percent can be characterized as "engaged" employees.[25] In contrast, of those who disagreed that they could make the disclosure, only 18.5 percent were engaged, and of those who neither agreed nor disagreed that a disclosure could be made without personal consequences, only 39.3 percent were engaged. A similar effect occurred for our survey questions about being actively encouraged to report wrongdoing and receiving praise for reporting wrongdoing. A culture that supports whistleblowing activities tends to also be a culture that fosters engagement among employees.[26]

It is important to recognize that this culture is not just a result of the relationship between a supervisor and his or her employees. Coworkers can make an employee's life easier or harder as well, and a spirit of cooperation and teamwork is one of the factors used by MSPB to measure engagement. It is therefore important that management create a culture where employees will not be shunned by their peers for coming forward with reports of wrongdoing.

We also asked respondents how adequate they believed the protections against reprisal were for Federal employees who report wrongdoing. More than 50 percent stated that they believed the protections were adequate, while 28 percent said the protections were inadequate, and 20 percent indicated that they considered the protections neither adequate nor inadequate. It is unclear how well respondents understand the protections available to them. However, with more than a quarter of respondents believing the protections are inadequate, there is a potential that, to the extent that a fear of retaliation plays a role in the decision to blow the whistle, perceptions of inadequate protections could discourage employees from reporting wrongdoing.

As indicated earlier in this chapter, concern about retaliation is often not the most important consideration for most employees when deciding to disclose wrongdoing, but this concern still can play a substantial role. Educating employees about their rights may help dispel some concerns and thereby encourage more disclosures. Additionally, such education also may persuade employees that the agency will not want to retaliate against employees who come forward with reports of wrongdoing. On its face, an agency that wants employees to know their rights simply appears less likely to be an agency that is interested in violating those rights. Improving the agency's culture is one more reason to ensure that the training mandated by the No Fear Act is provided effectively.

Whom to Tell About Wrongdoing and Preserving Anonymity

We asked respondents: "If you were to observe or have evidence of wrongdoing, how important would it be to you that you be able to report it without disclosing your identity?" Eighty percent of respondents indicated that anonymity would be either important or very important to them. The information provided to us by OIGs also indicates that anonymity is important. As one OIG put it, "it encourages reporting and makes retaliation nearly impossible." But, anonymity and confidentiality are not easy to achieve, and not all entities are trusted to the same degree.

Whom to Tell

We asked respondents to what extent they believed that various organizations would keep their identity a secret if the respondent asked for confidentiality. We also asked about the extent to which the respondents believed that organizations would take the reports seriously, given the emphasis that respondents placed on whether something would be done about the wrongdoing when deciding to make a disclosure. The results, shown in figure 5, below, show a higher level of confidence in Federal agencies than in Congress or the media.

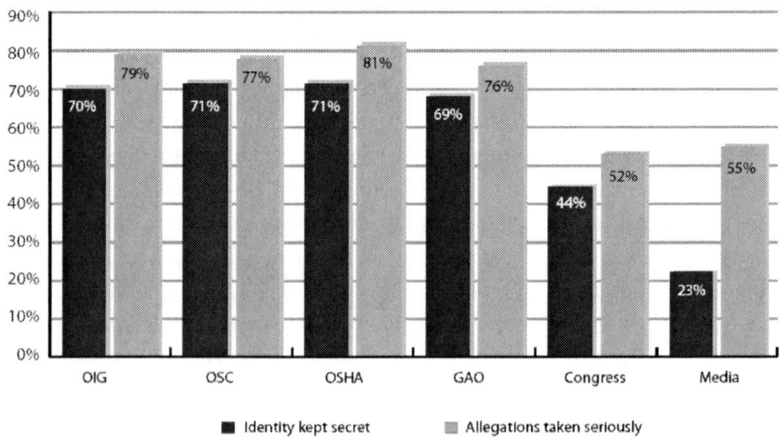

Figure 5. Percentage of respondents indicating their level of trust in various agencies, organizations, or institutions.

It is worth noting that this is a survey of Federal employees in the Executive branch. It may well be that these respondents—as civil servants—have a strong and invested opinion regarding how hard working and dedicated most civil servants are. This could cause the respondents to be more inclined to trust Federal employees assigned with investigating wrongdoing to act professionally, both with regard to taking any allegations seriously and preserving confidentiality.

In contrast, the U.S. Congress and the media were not held in high regard in 2010 among the American people as a whole. In the summer of 2010, at approximately the same time that our survey was administered, a Gallup poll showed that only 11 percent of the public had confidence in Congress, and 22-25 percent had confidence in television news and newspapers, respectively.[27]

Just as managers cannot expect employees to entrust them with disclosures of wrongdoing if the employees do not have confidence in them, a low approval rating for Congress and the media may have a relationship to the willingness of individuals to trust Congress or the media to respect a request for confidentiality or to take allegations seriously. It is particularly interesting that the media had the lowest levels of trust in confidentiality, given the journalistic concept of protecting a source and the fact that some American journalists have gone to prison to protect a source from being named. While the media is not a branch of the government, it is, nevertheless, an important player in exposing wrongdoing, both inside and outside the government.

Preserving Anonymity

Unfortunately, while anonymity is important to most employees, making an anonymous disclosure can be difficult. OSC will not accept anonymous disclosures, although agency OIGs will.[28] Even if an individual contacts an OIG and does not provide his or her name, it can be problematic to maintain anonymity. As one OIG put it, the "OIG's ability to allow whistleblowers to remain anonymous is frequently rendered ineffective by the malefactors' ability to use circumstantial evidence to determine the identity of the discloser."

We asked OIGs what could be done to better preserve anonymity. ***The Board does not endorse any particular approach to this issue. We only share this information to help the reader understand the difficulties with anonymous reports and what OIGs, as experts in disclosures and investigations, shared with us.*** One OIG recommended that the individual making a report contact the OIG anonymously, provide in the report as many details as possible that are known by multiple parties, and include a list of names of potential candidates for further information to be contacted by the OIG. The individual could plant his or her name among the many names provided. In that way, the individual could make it possible for the OIG to gather needed information and if anything in the report of investigation could be tracked back to the individual as the sole party with the information, it would appear that the discloser was *forced* to provide the information as a part of an agency investigation rather than be seen as the instigator of the investigation.[29]

Another OIG recommended against anonymity if the employee has already brought his or her concerns to management's attention, or if the allegations the employee presents are known to only a handful of individuals. Under these conditions, this OIG recommended that the individual sign a consent form giving OIG permission to release his or her identity, as that could potentially make future retaliation against the employee easier to prove as whistleblower retaliation because the individual would be better able to establish that the officials not only might have suspected but actually knew that the individual was the one who made the disclosure to the OIG.[30]

Disclosures Matter

When the CSRA was first enacted, it was noted that:

> In the vast Federal bureaucracy it is not difficult to conceal wrongdoing provided that no one summons the courage to disclose the truth. Whenever misdeeds take place in a Federal agency, there are employees who know that it has occurred, and who are outraged by it. What is needed is a means to assure them that they will not suffer if they help uncover and correct administrative abuses.[31]

We asked OIGs how important disclosures from current or former employees of the agency are when it comes to the OIGs' ability to identify and investigate illegal activities, fraud, waste, or abuse. We also inquired why the disclosures were important. Their comments indicated that the disclosures were at least somewhat useful, and the overwhelming majority of comments indicated that the disclosures were very important. Many OIGs stated that the disclosures had led to successful criminal prosecutions and cost savings. Below are a few examples of the comments that we received:

- Employee disclosures are very important. The most significant efforts made by my agency during the past year were based, initially, on the reports of an anonymous whistleblower.
- Disclosures have been the number one source of information leading to the identification and investigation of illegal activities, fraud, waste, and abuse.
- Disclosures from current or former employees have been critical to many of our investigations, as in many instances only current or former employees would possess the pertinent information.

- Disclosures from current or former employees are very important. They are closest to the work and have the most opportunity to identify fraud... Some of our largest cases, dollar-wise and impact-wise, have been from employee referrals.
- Disclosures and complaints to the Hotline serve as a primary source of identification and investigations of fraud, waste, abuse and wrongdoing. These disclosures are important because the individuals making them often have firsthand knowledge, insight, and investigative leads that will assist in any IG effort.

Employees are the most valuable asset that agencies have to reduce fraud, waste, and abuse. As shown throughout this chapter, factors related to an agency's culture tend to be important to employees when they decide whether to report wrongdoing that they have observed. We therefore encourage agencies to do more to create a culture that encourages employees to come forward with valuable information that could make the agencies more effective and efficient. As one OIG put it, "a culture committed to supporting employees who blow the whistle or report fraud, waste and abuse coupled with meaningful enforcement against the retaliator will go a long way to improving reporting and enhancing the well-being of the civil service."

CONCLUSION

We have seen some progress in the Federal Government with respect to effectively utilizing Federal employees to reduce or prevent fraud, waste, and abuse. Since 1992, the percentage of employees who perceive any wrongdoing has decreased, and for those who perceive wrongdoing, the frequency with which they observe the wrongdoing has also decreased. Additionally, in comparison to 1992, respondents in 2010 were slightly more likely to report the wrongdoing and less likely to think they have been identified as the source of the report.

However, among those individuals who indicated that they reported the wrongdoing and were identified as the source of the report, the potential for retaliation remains a serious problem, with approximately one-third of such respondents in both 1992 and 2010 perceiving either threats or acts of reprisal, or both.

Furthermore, when wrongdoing occurs, it is expensive, perhaps more so now than in 1992. So, while progress has been made to reduce wrongdoing, it is more important than ever that employees report wrongdoing when it does occur.

In 1978, Congress enacted a law to protect whistleblowers, and then amended that law in 1989 and 1994 to strengthen those protections. However, the percentage of individuals who perceived that they were retaliated against after being identified as whistleblowers has not changed substantially since 1992. The law contains what some perceive as substantial gaps in protection. In recent years, Congress has considered enacting further amendments to provide employees with better protection from retaliation. However, even if amended, laws to protect employees from retaliation can go only so far in encouraging reports of wrongdoing because a fear of retaliation for whistleblowing activity is only one of many factors that can influence an employee's decision to report wrongdoing.

Ultimately, the best way to ensure that employees will report wrongdoing is a combination of: (1) creating agency cultures that encourage whistleblowing by making it clear that management wants to stop wrongdoing, and (2) providing legal protections for whistleblowers who experience retaliation or threats of retaliation.

Whistleblower protection laws are necessary to encourage employees to report wrongdoing. While notable progress has been made in educating employees about their rights under the law with respect to protection from reprisal, training in this area can and should be improved. However, in the end, the redress for whistleblowing retaliation will not affect disclosures of wrongdoing as much as a culture in which employees believe that their whistleblowing will make a real difference. From the President and the Congress, to the agency leaders they nominate and confirm, and down through the ranks of the career civil service, we encourage all of those in a position of influence to set the tone that reporting wrongdoing is a public service and a public duty and that retaliation against whistleblowers will not be tolerated. The law is important, but the law cannot do it alone.

Appendix: 1992 and 2010 MPS Data for Whistleblowing

As mentioned earlier, MSPB has been conducting Government-wide surveys at regular intervals for nearly 30 years. In 1992, a large portion of our MPS survey was dedicated to issues related to whistleblowing and whistleblower retaliation. For our 2010 MPS, we deliberately asked several of the same questions we asked in 1992 to see if the passage of eighteen years and amendments to the Whistleblower Protection Act in 1994 had any discernable impact.[32] We remind readers that survey data includes a margin for error, and small differences in data should not be given too much importance. Furthermore, there are myriad factors that can influence data, including the fact that the Federal workforce and the work it performs has changed greatly over the past eighteen years. However, the data is presented below, side by side, for comparison.

1992	2010	
During the last 12 months, did you personally observe or obtain direct evidence of one or more illegal or wasteful activities involving your agency? (Note: Do not answer "yes" if you only read about the activity in the newspaper or heard about it as a rumor.)		
17.7%	11.1%	Yes
82.3%	88.9%	No

1992	2010	
If you answered yes to the question above, then please select the activity below that represents the most serious problem you personally observed. (Please mark only one.)		
1.9%	1.8%	Stealing Federal funds
6.3%	3.1%	Stealing Federal property
0.2%	0.2%	Accepting bribes or kickbacks
5.0%	5.1%	Waste caused by ineligible people receiving funds, goods, or services
17.9%	13.8%	Waste caused by unnecessary or deficient goods or services
11.9%	10.1%	Use of an official position for personal benefit
35.3%	38.9%	Waste caused by a badly managed program
3.9%	4.8%	Unfair advantage in the selection of a contractor, consultant, or vendor
4.8%	4.6%	Tolerating a situation or practice which poses a substantial and specific danger to public health or safety
13.0%	17.6%	Other serious violation of law or regulation

Where did this activity occur or originate? (Please mark ALL that apply.)		
43.8%	48.5%	Your workgroup
64.2%	49.4%	Outside your workgroup, but within your agency
5.4%	3.3%	Another Federal agency
12.2%	8.1%	Contractor or vendor
2.4%	4.5%	Other
If a dollar value can be placed on this activity, what was the amount involved?		
4.1%	2.2%	Less than $100
10.8%	5.5%	$100-$999
13.6%	7.6%	$1,000-$4,999
28.0%	34.7%	$5,000-$100,000
23.0%	34.5%	More than $100,000
20.5%	15.5%	A dollar value cannot be placed on the activity

1992	2010	
How frequently did this activity occur?		
12.8%	14.1%	Once or rarely
33.0%	27.2%	Occasionally
46.0%	44.4%	Frequently
8.2%	14.3%	Don't know/Can't judge

Did you report this activity to any of the following? (Please mark ALL that apply.)		
39.8%	35.0%	I did not report the activity
26.6%	20.5%	Family member or friend
37.1%	35.9%	Co-worker
35.9%	33.4%	Immediate supervisor
20.2%	19.9%	Higher level supervisor
8.0%	8.6%	Higher level agency official
5.6%	5.1%	Agency Inspector General
0.7%	1.1%	Office of Special Counsel
0.3%	0.6%	Government Accountability Office
2.7%	1.5%	Law enforcement official
5.7%	7.2%	Union representative
0.2%	0.6%	News media
1.9%	1.8%	Congressional staff member or member of Congress
0.7%	0.6%	Advocacy group outside the Government
3.8%	8.8%	Other

1992	2010	
If you DID report this activity, were you identified as the source of the report		
53.1%	42.5%	Yes, I was identified
46.9%	57.5%	No, I was not identified

If you were identified, what was the effect on you personally as a result of being identified? (Please mark ALL that apply.)		
9.2%	7.1%	I was given credit by my management for having reported the problem
37.2%	44.0%	Nothing happened to me for having reported the problem
18.4%	17.6%	My coworkers were unhappy with me for having reported the problem
31.2%	28.6%	My supervisor was unhappy with me for having reported the problem
35.8%	28.0%	Someone above my supervisor was unhappy with me for having reported the problem
12.2%	13.3%	I was threatened with reprisal for having reported the problem
18.7%	21.6%	I received an actual reprisal for having reported the problem

Within the last 12 months, have you personally experienced some type of reprisal or threat of reprisal by management for having reported an activity?		
36.3%	35.9%	Yes
63.7%	64.1%	No

1992		2010		
Did the reprisal or threat of reprisal take any of the following forms? (Please mark ALL that apply.)				
Threatened	Experienced	Threatened	Experienced	
11.8%	48.2%	10.8%	50.3%	Poor performance appraisal
5.1%	18.5%	10.3%	38.9%	Denial of promotion
1.5%	19.0%	6.6%	39.8%	Denial of opportunity for training
2.6%	30.7%	8.4%	46.8%	Denial of award
8.0%	36.1%	9.3%	45.9%	Assignment to less desirable or less important duties
3.8%	22.9%	6.1%	29.1%	Transfer or reassignment to a different job with less desirable duties

(Continued)

1992		2010		
Did the reprisal or threat of reprisal take any of the following forms? (Please mark ALL that apply.)				
Threatened	Experienced	Threatened	Experienced	
3.1%	5.2%	7.1%	13.7%	Reassignment to a different geographical location
3.3%	2.5%	6.8%	14.7%	Suspension from my job
1.9%	0.7%	9.1%	8.9%	Fired from my job
3.9%	3.1%	3.6%	14.8%	Grade level demotion
3.1%	48.8%	9.1%	63.5%	Shunned by coworkers or managers
8.7%	47.6%	11.9%	54.3%	Verbal harassment or intimidation
2.0%	1.6%	1.4%	6.1%	Required to take a fitness for duty exam
5.3%	14.5%	8.0%	32.7%	Other

1992	2010	
In response to the reprisal or threat of reprisal, did you take any of the following actions? (Please mark ALL that apply.)		
45.2%	26.4%	Took no action
36.2%	37.6%	Complained to a higher level of agency management
8.4%	15.6%	Complained to the Office of Inspector General within agency
31.8%	29.9%	Complained to some other office within agency (for example, the Personnel Office or EEO Office)
17.3%	20.3%	Filed a complaint through union representative
12.1%	14.9%	Filed a formal grievance within agency
16.2%	23.7%	Filed an EEO (discrimination) complaint
1.9%	9.2%	Filed a complaint with the Office of Special Counsel
1.7%	4.0%	Filed an action with the Merit Systems Protection Board
11.9%	18.4%	Took an action not listed above

How important, if at all, would each of the following be in encouraging you to report an illegal or wasteful activity?		
		The activity might endanger people's lives
95.7%	91.2%	Very Important
3.1%	6.0%	Somewhat Important
*	1.8%	Neither Important nor Unimportant
*	0.4%	Somewhat Unimportant
1.8%	0.7%	Unimportant**
		The activity was something you considered serious in terms of costs to the Government
66.5%	60.0%	Very Important
31.1%	32.4%	Somewhat Important
*	5.5%	Neither Important nor Unimportant
*	1.0%	Somewhat Unimportant
2.4%	1.2%	Unimportant**

* This response option was not offered on the 1992 survey for this question.

** This option was phrased as "Not Important" on the 1992 survey.

1992	2010	
How important, if at all, would each of the following be in encouraging you to report an illegal or wasteful activity? (Continued)		
		Something would be done to correct the activity you reported
69.2%	57.4%	Very Important
27.7%	32.6%	Somewhat Important
*	7.6%	Neither Important nor Unimportant
*	0.9%	Somewhat Unimportant
3.6%	1.6%	Unimportant**
		The wrongdoers involved in the activities would be punished
41.5%	38.3%	Very Important
38.0%	33.1%	Somewhat Important
*	21.4%	Neither Important nor Unimportant
*	3.0%	Somewhat Unimportant
14.5%	4.3%	Unimportant**
		You would be protected from any sort of reprisal
68.8%	59.3%	Very Important
23.8%	2.5%	Somewhat Important
*	10.3%	Neither Important nor Unimportant
*	1.7%	Somewhat Unimportant

(Continued)

1992	2010	
How important, if at all, would each of the following be in encouraging you to report an illegal or wasteful activity? (Continued)		
7.4%	3.1%	Unimportant**
		You would be positively recognized by management for a good deed
22.2%	16.8%	Very Important
23.2%	17.4%	Somewhat Important
*	39.1%	Neither Important nor Unimportant
*	5.9%	Somewhat Unimportant
54.7%	20.8%	Unimportant**

* This response option was not offered on the 1992 survey for this question.

** This option was phrased as “Not Important” on the 1992 survey.

1992	2010	
		Your identity would be kept confidential by the people to whom you reported the activity
55.4%	52.6%	Very Important
28.7%	26.9%	Somewhat Important
*	13.7%	Neither Important nor Unimportant
*	2.9%	Somewhat Unimportant
15.9%	3.9%	Unimportant**
		The activity was something you considered to be a serious ethical violation, although the monetary costs associated with it were small
50.1%	48.5%	Very Important
41.3%	33.3%	Somewhat Important
*	12.5%	Neither Important nor Unimportant
*	1.6%	Somewhat Unimportant
7.8%	4.0%	Unimportant**
		You would be eligible to receive a cash award
9.6%	6.7%	Very Important
18.6%	8.9%	Somewhat Important
*	37.0%	Neither Important nor Unimportant
*	4.0%	Somewhat Unimportant
71.8%	42.5%	Unimportant**

* This response option was not offered on the 1992 survey for this question.

** This option was phrased as “Not Important” on the 1992 survey.

1992	2010	
How likely would you be to "blow the whistle" when the wrongdoer is:		
		Your supervisor
28.0%	30.1%	Very Likely
34.7%	31.8%	Somewhat Likely
*	16.4%	Neither Likely nor Unlikely
16.9%	8.0%	Somewhat Unlikely
11.5%	6.0%	Very Unlikely
8.9%	7.8%	Don't Know/Can't Judge
		A higher level supervisor
30.9%	32.1%	Very Likely
34.2%	31.2%	Somewhat Likely
*	15.9%	Neither Likely nor Unlikely
14.8%	6.9%	Somewhat Unlikely
11.9%	6.2%	Very Unlikely
8.4%	7.7%	Don't Know/Can't Judge
		A coworker (in your work group)
29.7%	32.1%	Very Likely
40.9%	36.0%	Somewhat Likely
*	16.7%	Neither Likely nor Unlikely
15.3%	5.5%	Somewhat Unlikely
6.4%	2.7%	Very Unlikely
7.6%	6.9%	Don't Know/Can't Judge

* This response option was not offered on the 1992 survey for this question.

1992	2010	
		A Federal employee outside your work group
39.6%	38.5%	Very Likely
37.4%	34.1%	Somewhat Likely
*	14.6%	Neither Likely nor Unlikely
9.7%	2.9%	Somewhat Unlikely
5.1%	2.3%	Very Unlikely
8.2%	7.6%	Don't Know/Can't Judge
		A contractor or vendor
59.4%	50.3%	Very Likely
25.6%	28.2%	Somewhat Likely
*	11.0%	Neither Likely nor Unlikely
4.3%	1.4%	Somewhat Unlikely
3.2%	1.8%	Very Unlikely
7.4%	7.2%	Don't Know/Can't Judge

(Continued)

1992	2010	
		A political appointee in your agency
49.1%	41.8%	Very Likely
25.5%	26.4%	Somewhat Likely
*	13.8%	Neither Likely nor Unlikely
6.2%	2.6%	Somewhat Unlikely
6.3%	3.5%	Very Unlikely
12.9%	11.8%	Don't Know/Can't Judge

*This response option was not offered on the 1992 survey for this question.

End Notes

[1] 5 U.S.C. § 2302(b)(8)(A). For ease of reference, throughout this report, a violation of any law, rule, or regulation, or gross mismanagement, a gross waste of funds, an abuse of authority, or a substantial and specific danger to public health or safety may be referred to as "wrongdoing."

[2] The survey data discussed in this report are from a survey of more than 13,000 Federal employees in 1992, and a survey of more than 40,000 Federal employees in 2010. Both surveys were conducted by the U.S. Merit Systems Protection Board based on random samples drawn from the Office of Personnel Management's Central Personnel Data File.

[3] As explained in our recent report, *Whistleblower Protections for Federal Employees*, available at www.mspb.gov/studies, not all reports of wrongdoing are protected disclosures, and not all unpleasant reactions by the agency constitute retaliation as defined by the law.

[4] 5 U.S.C. § 2302(b)(8)(A). The law also protects individuals from an agency's failure to take a personnel action, or threats to take or not take a personnel action, if the agency's conduct is because of the disclosure of wrongdoing.

[5] 5 U.S.C. § 1204(a)(3).

[6] 5 U.S.C. § 2301(b)(4). It is also a basic obligation of public service that "[e]mployees shall disclose waste, fraud, abuse, and corruption to appropriate authorities." 5 C.F.R. § 2635.101(b)(11).

[7] *Whistleblower Protections for Federal Employees*, available at www.mspb.gov/studies.

[8] The electronic version of the survey was offered to 70,675 employees, with 41,680 respondents, for a response rate of 59 percent. The paper version of the survey was mailed to 1,295 employees from the Federal Aviation Administration, with 340 surveys returned, for a response rate of 26 percent.

[9] Because our 1992 survey used the term "report" to describe the act of telling others about wrongdoing, we opted to use that term for the 2010 survey as well. However, when it comes to protecting whistleblowers, the Federal Circuit has held that it is *disclosures* that are protected, not reports. *See Huffman v. Office of Personnel Management*, 263 F.3d 1341, 1349-50 (Fed. Cir. 2001) (holding that "[w]hen an employee reports or states that there has been misconduct by a wrongdoer to the wrongdoer, the employee is not making a 'disclosure' of misconduct" and the Whistleblower Protection Act will not apply. This is

because "the term 'disclosure' means to reveal something that was hidden and not known. It is also quite significant that Congress in the WPA did not use a word with a broader connotation such as 'report' or 'state.'")

[10] Margin of error is a statistic that is used when a random sample is drawn to represent a larger population. It reflects how much the data provided may differ from what would be obtained if every individual in the larger population had been asked the same question.

[11] Because we are drilling down into increasingly smaller segments of our respondents throughout this chapter, and using data from two separate administrations of the survey, there is no single, consistent, margin for error. It can be as much as +/- 5 percent, with a confidence interval of 95 percent. This means we can be 95 percent sure that the data we provide in this chapter is within 5 percent of the data that would be obtained if we posed the question to all Federal employees.

[12] 5 U.S.C. § 2302(b)(8). There are also additional conditions that must be met in order to make a disclosure protected. For more on protected disclosures, see our report, *Whistleblower Protections for Federal Employees*, available at www.mpsb.gov/studies.

[13] Government Executive, *OMB Sets Standards for Contracting Officials*, available at http://www.govexec.com/ dailyfed/1107/113007e1.htm. For more on contracting officers and their technical advisors, *see Contracting Officer Representatives: Managing the Government's Technical Experts to Achieve Positive Contract Outcomes*, available at www. mspb.gov/studies.

[14] Not all wrongdoing can be financially quantified. However, the percentage of respondents who stated that a dollar value could not be placed on the activity dropped from 21 percent in 1992 to 16 percent in 2010.

[15] The specific facts of the case will determine whether a report of wrongdoing to an individual in one or more of these groups constitutes a protected disclosure. For example, in *Parikh v. Department of Veterans Affairs*, 116 M.S.P.R. 197 (2011), a physician disclosed patient medical records to various Members of Congress as well as others, outside of the Government, in order to draw attention to what he perceived as poor medical treatment for veterans. In this particular case, giving the information to members of Congress was a protected disclosure, while providing the information to others was not protected.

[16] 5 U.S.C. § 2302(b)(8).

[17] 5 U.S.C. § 2302(a)(2)(A); *see Whistleblower Protections for Federal Employees*, p. 34, available at www.mspb. gov; 5 U.S.C. § 2302(a)(2)(A).

[18] Not all forms of reprisal in this table are considered "personnel actions" under the law; the Whistleblower Protection Act's coverage is limited to personnel actions. *See* 5 U.S.C. § 2302(a)(2)(A); *Whistleblowing Protections for Federal Employees*, available at www.mspb.gov/studies.

[19] While it is difficult to make further distinctions reliably when dealing with such a small population, it does not appear that gender, salary, or age influenced responses to the questions in table 6. The National Security Personnel System (NSPS) also does not appear to be a factor, as there was no substantive difference between the responses for Department of Defense (DOD) versus non DOD agencies.

[20] U.S. Merit Systems Protection Board, *Whistleblowing in the Federal Government: An Update* (1993) p. 37, available at www.mspb.gov/studies.

[21] *See* Notification and Federal Employee Antidiscrimination and Retaliation (No Fear) Act, P.L. 107-174, §§ 201-202.

[22] *Lachance v. White*, 174 F.3d 1378, 1381 (Fed. Cir. 1999) (holding that "the proper test is this: could a disinterested observer with knowledge of the essential facts known to and readily

ascertainable by the employee reasonably conclude" that wrongdoing as defined in 5 U.S.C. § 2302(b)(8) occurred?).

[23] *Huffman v. Office of Personnel Management*, 263 F.3d 1341, 1348 (Fed. Cir. 2001).

[24] *Prohibited Personnel Practices: Employee Perceptions*, available at www.mspb.gov/studies.

[25] Engaged employees have a heightened connection to their work, their organization, or the people they work for or with that causes them to produce better results for the organization. The greater an employee's engagement, the more likely it is that the employee will go above and beyond minimum requirements and expend discretionary effort to provide excellent performance. For more on engagement and MSPB's engagement index, *see* U.S. Merit Systems Protection Board, *The Power of Federal Engagement,* available at www.mpsb.gov/studies; *see also Managing for Engagement—Communication, Connection, and Courage*, available at www.mpsb.gov/studies.

[26] Retaliatory action because of whistleblowing activity is a prohibited personnel practice. As discussed in our recent report, *Prohibited Personnel Practices: Employee Perceptions*, available at www.mspb.gov/studies, employee perceptions of management committing prohibited personnel practices tends to correlate with low engagement.

[27] Gallup, "Congress Ranks Last in Confidence in Institutions," available at http://www.gallup.com/poll/141512/congress-ranks-last-confidence-institutions.aspx. Gallup's poll was conducted July 8-11, 2010. The MPS was conducted from July 15-September 24, 2010.

[28] Office of Special Counsel, http://www.osc.gov/wbdiscEval.htm. ("OSC will generally not consider anonymous disclosures. If a disclosure is filed by an anonymous source, the disclosure will be referred to the Office of Inspector General in the appropriate agency. OSC will take no further action on the disclosure.")

[29] An employee's failure to cooperate with an official investigation or lack of candor during an investigation can be grounds for an adverse action. *See Ludlum v. Department of Justice*, 278 F.3d 1280 (Fed. Cir. 2002); *Little v. Department of Transportation*, 112 M.S.P.R. 224 (2009); *Social Security Administration v. Steverson*, 111 M.S.P.R. 649 (2009); *Pedeleose v. Department of Defense*, 110 M.S.P.R. 508 (2009); *Jackson v. Department of the Army*, 99 M.S.P.R. 604 (2005).

[30] For more on the difficulties an employee may encounter when seeking protection against whistleblower retaliation, and using the knowledge/timing test as a means to establish retaliation, please see our recent report, *Whistleblower Protections for Federal Employees*, available at www.mspb.gov/studies.

[31] S. Rep. 95-969, 8 (1978 U.S.C.C.A.N. 2723, 2730). (This is the Senate Report that accompanied the Civil Service Reform Act of 1978.)

[32] For some questions, the order in which responses were offered to respondents was different in 2010 than it had been in 1992. For these questions, the order has been changed on this table to make comparing the two years easier.

In: Whistleblowing by Federal Employees ISBN: 978-1-63117-480-3
Editor: Bernard L. Gallagher

Chapter 2

WHISTLEBLOWER PROTECTIONS FOR FEDERAL EMPLOYEES*

U.S. Merit Systems Protection Board

September 2010

The President
President of the Senate
Speaker of the House of Representatives

Dear Sirs and Madam:

In accordance with the requirements of 5 U.S.C. § 1204(a)(3), it is my honor to submit this U.S. Merit Systems Protection Board report, *Whistleblower Protections for Federal Employees*. The purpose of this report is to describe the requirements for a Federal employee's disclosure of wrongdoing to be legally protected as whistleblowing under current statutes and case law.

To qualify as a protected whistleblower, a Federal employee or applicant for employment must disclose: a violation of any law, rule, or regulation; gross mismanagement; a gross waste of funds; an abuse of authority; or a substantial and specific danger to public health or safety. However, this disclosure alone

* This is an edited, reformatted and augmented version of a report to the President and Congress from the U.S. Merit Systems Protection Board, dated September 2010.

is not enough to obtain protection under the law. The individual also must: avoid using normal channels if the disclosure is in the course of the employee's duties; make the report to someone other than the wrongdoer; and suffer a personnel action, the agency's failure to take a personnel action, or the threat to take or not take a personnel action. Lastly, the employee must seek redress through the proper channels before filing an appeal with the U.S. Merit Systems Protection Board ("MSPB"). A potential whistleblower's failure to meet even one of these criteria will deprive the MSPB of jurisdiction, and render us unable to provide any redress in the absence of a different (non-whistleblowing) appeal right.

This report spells out in greater depth the difficulties a potential whistleblower may face when navigating the law to seek protection from agency retaliation. I hope you will find this report useful as you consider issues affecting the Government's ability to protect employees who disclose fraud, waste, abuse, and other wrongdoing within the Federal Government.

Respectfully,
Susan Tsui Grundmann

EXECUTIVE SUMMARY

There are certain personnel practices that are, by statute, forbidden in the Federal Government. They are known as the Prohibited Personnel Practices (PPPs). One of the most frequently discussed PPPs is the prohibition against retaliating against an employee for the act of disclosing a violation of any law, rule, or regulation; gross mismanagement; a gross waste of funds; an abuse of authority; or a substantial and specific danger to public health or safety.[1] In common parlance, such an employee is known as a whistleblower and acting against the employee because of the whistleblowing is whistleblower retaliation. However, the law can be quite different from common parlance. In the Federal Government, not everyone who discloses wrongdoing will be considered a whistleblower, and not every act of retaliation against a whistleblower is legally redressable.

The U.S. Merit Systems Protection Board ("MSPB" or "the Board") is charged by statute to help agencies prevent PPPs through the MSPB's adjudicatory and studies missions.[2] Through its adjudicatory mission, the MSPB rules upon cases within its jurisdiction and can order corrective action to undo the effect of a PPP. But, the MSPB will not automatically have jurisdiction over all allegations that a PPP has occurred. Instead, the MSPB has jurisdiction only after a series of conditions has been met. The PPP of whistleblower retaliation has a particularly complex set of requirements for jurisdiction.

Through its studies mission, the MSPB is charged to report to the President and Congress on whether the public's interest in a Government free from PPPs is being adequately protected. The MSPB has the authority to study any topic "relating to the civil service and to other merit systems in the executive branch[.]"[3] This report is one in a series of reports on the PPP of retaliation for whistleblowing and takes as its focus the law.[4] The purpose of this report is to help inform the public discussion regarding when the law does—and does not—protect those Federal employees who disclose wrongdoing in their agencies.

When a Federal employee or applicant discloses wrongdoing and believes that he or she has been retaliated against for the disclosure, in order to be potentially entitled to relief under the law, the individual must:

1) Disclose conduct that meets a specific category of wrongdoing set forth in the law.
2) Make the disclosure to the "right" type of party. Depending on the nature of the disclosure, the employee may be limited regarding to whom the report can be made.
3) Make a report that is either: (a) outside of the employee's course of duties; or (b) communicated outside of normal channels.
4) Make the report to someone other than the wrongdoer.
5) Have a reasonable belief of wrongdoing. The employee does not have to be *correct*, but the belief must be *reasonable* to a disinterested observer.
6) Suffer a personnel action, the agency's failure to take a personnel action, or the threat to take or not take a personnel action.[5]
7) Demonstrate a connection between the disclosure and the personnel action, failure to take a personnel action, or the threat to take or not take a personnel action.
8) Seek redress through the proper channels.[6]

However, even if a whistleblower establishes all of the above, the law states that the relief sought by the individual will not be ordered if the agency can establish by clear and convincing evidence that it would have taken the same action in the absence of the whistleblowing.[7]

INTRODUCTION

> "Often, the whistle blower's reward for dedication to the highest morale [sic] principles is harassment and abuse. Whistle blowers frequently encounter severe damage to their careers and substantial economic loss. Protecting employees who disclose government illegality, waste, and corruption is a major step toward a more effective civil service. In the vast Federal bureaucracy it is not difficult to conceal wrongdoing provided that no one summons the courage to disclose the truth. Whenever misdeeds take place in a Federal agency, there are employees who know that it has occurred, and who are outraged by it. What is needed is a means to assure them that they will not suffer if they help uncover and correct administrative abuses."[8]

Protecting whistleblowers was one of the goals of the Civil Service Reform Act (CSRA) of 1978. In the CSRA, Congress, for the first time, enacted a statute that was specifically intended to protect Federal employees from being punished for bringing wrongdoing to light. The statutory provisions for protecting whistleblowers, set forth in the CSRA, were amended in 1989 and again in 1994. In recent years, Congress has looked at the provisions and considered further amendments to strengthen the effectiveness of the law.

This report discusses what the law requires in order for a Federal employee to qualify as a whistleblower under legal precedents, and what the employee must do in order to receive protection from retaliation.[9] These statutory provisions are an attempt by the Congress to balance the needs of Federal agencies to manage their workforces effectively and the public's interest in having fraud, waste, abuse, illegalities, and public dangers exposed so that they can be addressed.

This report is presented as a part of the MSPB's statutory obligation to study and report upon prohibited personnel practices and the health of the merit systems. While we hope that this report will be useful to potential whistleblowers, their advocates, Federal agencies, the U.S. Congress, and the President, this report is not an official "opinion" of the Board in the adjudicatory sense.[10] We recommend that any party appearing before the MSPB rely directly upon the pertinent statutes, regulations, and legal precedents.

Because of the MSPB's role as the adjudicator of whistleblower retaliation claims, this report differs from most other reports issued under the MSPB's studies authority. Most MSPB studies include an evaluation of the information being provided and recommendations for the improvement of laws, regulations, managerial practices, or other aspects of the civil service in keeping with the merit principles. However, in order to preserve our neutrality as adjudicators, we have limited our evaluations in this particular report to those that are necessary to help the reader understand the information being provided, and we have not included recommendations for changes to Federal laws, regulations, or policies. The absence of recommendations in this report should not be interpreted as support for—or opposition to—any part of the laws as they are currently written, any decision by the Board or the Federal Circuit interpreting those laws, or any bill that seeks to amend the laws pertaining to Federal whistleblowers.

To make the discussion of whistleblowing easier in this report, we will define a violation of any law, rule, or regulation; gross mismanagement; a gross waste of funds; an abuse of authority; or a substantial and specific danger to public health or safety as "wrongdoing."[11] We will describe a person who seeks to disclose wrongdoing as a "potential whistleblower" and a person who is actually protected under the law, complete with jurisdiction to have a claim of retaliation heard by the U.S. Merit Systems Protection Board, as a "protected whistleblower." As this report will demonstrate, not every potential whistleblower is protected under the law.

A tear-out copy of some of the pertinent sections of the laws regarding whistleblowers is provided in the back of this report. *It is not a complete compilation of the law and should not be used other than in conjunction with this report.* However, the reader may wish to tear it out and have it available for easy reference when reading this report to help place the conversation in context.

A Brief History

When reading the current state of the law, it may be helpful to have a basic understanding of how the law came into being and the roles of the various actors involved in the process of evaluating whistleblower claims. This chapter provides a brief history for the sole purpose of context.

The OSC and the WPA

In the late 1970s, Congress and the President looked for ways to improve the civil service. The issue of whistleblowers within the Federal Government was a part of this discussion. Senator Patrick Leahy and his staff conducted a study of the whistleblowing issue in 1978 and submitted a report to the Committee on Governmental Affairs. This report noted that "[a]lthough statutes do exist which might be interpreted as applicable to whistleblower cases," the "Courts have been reluctant to play an active role in the whistleblower problem."[12]

In order to make the courts play an active role, Congress enacted the Civil Service Reform Act of 1978 (CSRA), which created specific statutory provisions that directly addressed the issue of retaliation against Federal employees who blow the whistle. For the first time, a Federal statute created a legal mandate within the civil service to protect whistleblowers from reprisal and to act against those who initiate reprisal actions.[13]

The CSRA created the Office of the Special Counsel (OSC) and placed it within the U.S. Merit Systems Protection Board. While the MSPB was the successor to the Civil Service Commission, and was tasked with adjudicating allegations of certain types of improper personnel actions, the Office of the Special Counsel was an entirely new concept. The role of OSC was to serve as a type of prosecutor. OSC's purpose was to receive and investigate allegations of prohibited personnel practices. OSC was authorized to seek remedial action from the MSPB to prevent abuses of the merit system, and to initiate disciplinary action against government officials who committed prohibited personnel practices. OSC was given a particular mandate to investigate and take action to prevent or correct reprisals against individuals who disclose agency wrongdoing.[14]

However, with regard to whistleblower protections, the result of the CSRA was not what Congress had hoped for. In particular, the Office of the Special Counsel was perceived as failing to protect whistleblowers. As a result, Congress passed the Whistleblower Protection Act (WPA) of 1989.

> The Whistleblower Protection Act was passed in 1989, in large part because the Office of Special Counsel was perceived as being ineffectual. At that time, OSC had not brought a single corrective action case since 1979 to the Merit Systems Protection Board on behalf of a whistleblower. A former Special Counsel had been quoted in the press advising whistleblowers 'Don't put your head up, because it will get blown off.' Whistleblowers told the

Governmental Affairs Committee that they thought of the OSC as an adversary, rather than an ally, and urged the Committee to abolish the office altogether.[15]

The WPA of 1989 separated OSC from the MSPB and made OSC its own, independent, Federal agency. The WPA of 1989 also created for the first time an individual right of action (IRA). As explained in greater depth later in this report, the IRA provides Federal employees with the legal standing to come before the MSPB with a complaint of whistleblower retaliation. Prior to the WPA of 1989, only OSC could bring such an action to the MSPB. Employees were limited to raising whistleblower reprisal as an affirmative defense in an otherwise appealable action.[16] In 1994, the WPA was amended, but many provisions remained the same.[17]

The Federal Circuit

The U.S. Court of Appeals for the Federal Circuit is the appeals court that reviews the decisions of the U.S. Merit Systems Protection Board. The Federal Circuit is unique among the Federal appeals courts because the 12 other Federal appeals courts each have authority over a specific geographic area. For example, a decision of a Federal District Court in California would go to the Ninth Circuit on appeal, while a decision on the exact same subject matter in a New York Federal District Court would go to the Second Circuit. In contrast, the Federal Circuit has no geographic limitations, but it has very limited subject matter jurisdiction. For most cases, no matter where in the world the case originates, if it falls under the jurisdiction of the MSPB, the Federal Circuit is the appeals court that will hear any appeal of the MSPB's decision.[18] The MSPB is bound by the decisions of the Federal Circuit.[19]

However, there are different types of decisions. In particular, a decision of the Federal Circuit may be precedential, or non-precedential. The term "table" often appears next the citation for non-precedential cases. The citation "Fed. Appx." also indicates a non-precedential case. These non-precedential decisions can be helpful because the court "may look to a nonprecedential disposition for guidance or persuasive reasoning[.]" However, the court "will not give one of its own nonprecedential dispositions the effect of binding precedent."[20]

In contrast, a precedential decision of the Federal Circuit can be overruled only by: (1) the Federal Circuit itself; (2) an amendment to the underlying statute that the opinion was based upon; or (3) a decision of the United States Supreme Court.[21] It is uncommon for the Federal Circuit to be overruled, but it has happened with regard to some whistleblower decisions, as will be discussed later in this report.

Requirements to Meet the Statutory Definition of a Whistleblower

Factors that can determine if someone is a whistleblower under the law can include: the type of information being disclosed; if the wrongdoing was reported to the "correct" party; if the wrongdoing was reported through the "correct" channels (which is situationally dependent); if there was no duty to report the information; if the individual was reasonable about being suspicious; if the wrongdoing reached a pre-determined (yet varied) level of seriousness; and if the wrongdoing was the sort of wrongdoing that Congress wanted to have covered under whistleblower laws. This chapter will discuss each of these requirements.

What Is Wrongdoing?

The law for Federal employees[22] defines a protected whistleblower as an employee or applicant who discloses information that he or she "reasonably believes evidences—

- a violation of any law, rule, or regulation, or
- gross mismanagement, a gross waste of funds, an abuse of authority, or a substantial and specific danger to public health or safety[.]"[23]

As noted above, there are several different categories of wrongdoing for which a report of the wrongdoing may constitute whistleblowing, such as violations of the law, mismanagement, fraud, waste, abuse of authority, etc. However, the categories are not all modified by the same words. These modifiers are important because they can determine if the conduct being reported is serious enough to qualify for protection. It is important to recognize that some conduct must be "gross" or "substantial" in order to qualify, while other conduct can qualify without meeting these criteria.

Violation of Any Law, Rule, or Regulation

Reporting a violation of any law, rule, or regulation potentially can qualify the employee for whistleblower status. However, while the violation of the law, rule, or regulation can be quite minor, the Federal Circuit has held that "disclosures of trivial violations do not constitute protected disclosures."[24] The Federal Circuit fortunately has provided a definition of what may constitute trivial. If the potential whistleblower is reporting what a reasonable person would consider "arguably minor and inadvertent miscues occurring in the conscientious carrying out of one's assigned duties[,]" then the disclosure is not protected.[25]

For example, in *Frederick v. Department of Justice*, a former Border Patrol agent (Womack) claimed that he had disclosed a violation of law by reporting that a fellow agent (Mayberry) allegedly violated international law by crossing the border into Mexico without Mexican permission. However, based upon testimony, it seemed that the exact location of the border was unclear. As a result, the court held even if the Mayberry had crossed over into Mexico, it was "such a minor transgression" that Womack could not have had a reasonable belief that Mayberry was violating a law, rule, or regulation within the meaning of the WPA. However, there have been numerous cases in which the Board or the Federal Circuit found that the potential wrongdoing in question was not minor or inadvertent, and thus disclosures of that activity were protected. For example, in *Lawley v. Department of the Treasury*, the Board held that a disclosure that employees in an agency training course had cheated on examinations could qualify as a disclosure because of a Federal regulation requiring that employees not engage in dishonest conduct.[26] In *Wojcicki v. Department of the Air Force*, the Board held that because there was a specific Occupational Safety and Health Administration (OSHA) regulation that applied to the situation being disclosed, a disclosure regarding a danger to safety could be protected as a disclosure of a violation of a regulation, regardless of whether it qualified as a substantial and specific danger to public safety.[27] In *Grubb v. Department of the Interior*, the Board held that disclosures regarding potential violations of the Federal Oil and Gas Royalty Management Act of 1982 and regarding time and attendance report falsification could be protected disclosures.[28] In *Drake v. Agency for International Development*, the Federal Circuit held that a disclosure of what was perceived by the employee as excessive drinking could be a protected disclosure because the agency conceded that the Department of State's Foreign Affairs Manual addressing such drinking was a law, rule, or regulation under the WPA.[29]

When "making a disclosure involving a violation of law, rule, or regulation, it is not necessary that the disclosure specify a particular kind of fraud, waste, or abuse that the WPA was intended to reach[.]"[30] Likewise, the specific law, rule, or regulation does not have to be cited by the employee, provided that there was sufficient information in the disclosure to indicate that a law, rule, or regulation was violated.[31] In particular, some allegations of wrongdoing, "such as theft of government property or fraudulent claims for pay, so obviously implicate a violation of law, rule, or regulation, that an appellant need not identify any particular law, rule, or regulation."[32]

Abuse of Authority

The term "an abuse of authority" also does not have a qualifier such as "gross," and therefore a disclosure may qualify for whistleblower protection even if the abuse is not substantial.[33] The meaning of "abuse of authority" is not defined in the statute, and the Board has held that the legislative history for the CSRA is silent on the question. The Board has therefore adopted a regulatory definition.[34] An abuse of authority requires an "arbitrary or capricious exercise of power by a federal official or employee that adversely affects the rights of any person or that results in personal gain or advantage to himself or to preferred other persons."[35]

Examples of conduct that the Board has held could *potentially* rise to the level of an abuse of authority include: harassment or intimidation of other employees;[36] assigning a grievance to a management official named as a subject in the grievance;[37] providing preferential treatment to an employee with whom the supervisor was perceived as having an intimate relationship;[38] or a decision to disqualify applicants because of their failure to submit documents that the agency had not requested.[39] In contrast, the Board has held— under the particular circumstances presented in certain cases—that it could not reasonably be considered an abuse of authority for management to: delay in taking a disciplinary action;[40] change an employee's performance appraisal plan;[41] or close a particular office even though the closure could cause employees to be disadvantaged for promotions.[42]

Gross Mismanagement or Gross Waste of Funds

In contrast to the provisions regarding violations of the law or abuse of authority, the statute contains the qualifying language "gross" when referring to disclosures about mismanagement or a waste of funds.[43] In order to qualify as gross, the agency's decision cannot be a debatable difference of opinion. The agency's ability to accomplish its mission must be implicated.[44] If the potential whistleblower reports mismanagement or a waste of funds where the wisdom of the management decision is open to debate, or the risk to the agency is too small, the employee may be unprotected.[45]

The Federal Circuit and the Board have held that gross mismanagement "does not include management decisions which are merely debatable, nor does it mean action or inaction which constitutes simple negligence or wrongdoing... Gross mismanagement means a management action or inaction which creates a substantial risk of significant adverse impact upon the agency's ability to accomplish its mission."[46] The actions of the agency must be so serious "that a conclusion the agency erred is not debatable among reasonable people."[47] For example, a management decision not to investigate "large-scale" thefts at a commissary and not to redeem $90,000 worth of coupons was deemed to constitute gross mismanagement.[48]

Mismanagement questions often involve issues related to how the workforce is treated or utilized. While some management decisions regarding the use of the workforce have been found to qualify as gross mismanagement, others have been held to be merely debatable differences of opinion. The key is the impact on the mission. For example, in *Swanson v. General Services Administration*, the Board held that if a manager "undermined the ability of " an office "to perform its mission by drastically cutting the number of employees, a reasonable person could conclude that" there had been gross mismanagement.[49] In contrast, when an employee disclosed his opinion that a few positions (including his own) should not be abolished, the Board held it was not a disclosure of gross mismanagement because mission failure was not implicated.[50]

A gross waste of funds "constitutes a more than debatable expenditure that is significantly out of proportion to the benefit reasonably expected to accrue to the government[.]"[51] For example, an agency's decision to accept products from a subcontractor that the potential whistleblower believed were not acceptable did not rise to the level of a gross waste of funds when the employee "offered no evidence to show how the subcontractor's performance adversely impacted the agency's ability to accomplish its mission."[52]

In contrast, the Board held that it was reasonable for an employee to believe that he was disclosing a gross waste of funds when he disclosed to an Inspector General that his agency had spent $15,000 to purchase a fuel management system that replaced a working system that provided all the same information.[53] Likewise, an allegation that an agency paid "a full complement of staff" at a facility after it had "markedly decreased its workload" there, and that these workers "could have easily been reassigned to another busy facility where the agency improperly employed extra staff that would have otherwise not been needed" constituted a non-frivolous allegation of a gross waste of funds.[54]

A Substantial and Specific Danger to Public Health or Safety

A danger to public health or safety also carries with it a qualifier. The danger must be substantial and specific in order for the report to fall under the whistleblower provisions.

> A variety of factors... determine when a disclosed danger is sufficiently substantial and specific to warrant protection under the WPA. One such factor is the likelihood of harm resulting from the danger. If the disclosed danger could only result in harm under speculative or improbable conditions, the disclosure should not enjoy protection. Another important factor is when the alleged harm may occur. A harm likely to occur in the immediate or near future should identify a protected disclosure much more than a harm likely to manifest only in the distant future. Both of these factors affect the specificity of the alleged danger, while the nature of the harm—the potential consequences—affects the substantiality of the danger.[55]

In its 2010 decision in *Chambers v. Department of the Interior*, the Federal Circuit held that when National Park Police Chief Teresa Chambers disclosed to the media information that traffic accidents had increased on the Baltimore-Washington ("BW") Parkway as a result of staffing shortages, the disclosure qualified as a substantial and specific danger to public safety. The disclosure qualified because: (1) the disclosure was specific about the source of the problem (there were two officers instead of the recommended four officers patrolling); (2) a specific consequence of the shortage was described (accidents); (3) motor vehicle accidents are a significant and serious danger to public safety; and (4) it was not a vague or speculative outcome—accidents had already happened as a result of the shortage. "Such specificity is sufficient to establish a disclosure meriting protection under the WPA."[56]

Similarly, in *Miller v. Department of Homeland Security*, the Board held that when an employee disclosed his reasonable belief that a machine designed to detect explosives in luggage failed 10 percent of the time, it qualified as a disclosure of a specific and substantial danger because "the potential consequences—placement of an explosive device on a commercial airliner—obviously would be catastrophic. Moreover, the extensive screening measures that have been put in place by the government to prevent such an occurrence are a reflection of how likely and imminent the threat may be."[57]

In contrast, there was not a specific and substantial danger when an employee informed the Inspector General's office that "the agency lacked ammunition and therefore instructed its Security Guards to not fully load their weapons" and to carry only six shotgun shells with them instead of the 25 shells the employee alleged they were supposed to carry. The employee asserted that "the Security Guards' lives and the lives of those they protected could have been in danger if they were attacked because their weapons were not fully loaded." However, the Board held that this "disclosure involved speculation that there could possibly be danger at some point in the future[,]" but the danger was not imminent. It was therefore an unprotected disclosure.[58]

While there are a number of factors related to how substantial and specific a danger must be in order for a disclosure of that danger to qualify as a protected disclosure, a disclosure of a danger to public health or safety does not have to affect the *general* public in order to be protected.[59] For example, in *Wojcicki v. Department of the Air Force*, an employee reported to his supervisor and other managers that he believed there was something wrong with a sandblasting protection device, causing he and his coworkers to be exposed to toxic dust. He believed this was the reason why he had begun to cough up blood. The Board held that the danger was "substantial because it affects the appellant as well as several co-workers who perform sandblasting, and because the harm that the appellant claims already occurred to him (the coughing up of blood), by almost any standard, would be considered abnormal, serious, and substantial." Therefore, "even though this appellant's disclosure about the sandblasting operation may have concerned a matter that affected only a limited number of co-workers, and even though it may have concerned a matter personal to him, it is still a protected whistleblowing disclosure."[60]

Criterion for Wrongdoing Summary

As illustrated above, for certain types of wrongdoing, the offense may be rather minor, and yet the reporting can be protected; while for other offenses, the wrongdoing must meet a higher level of seriousness before protection will result for the potential whistleblower. For example, a relatively minor violation of a regulation may result in a protected disclosure—even if there is absolutely no danger to anyone's physical safety—while a physical danger that is not covered by a regulation could require a rather immediate likelihood of harm. For the potential whistleblower who simply wants to prevent anyone from getting hurt, these distinctions may be very frustrating. Yet, it is important that potential whistleblowers be aware that the law contains these distinctions because the Board and courts must apply them and the distinctions can determine if a disclosure will be legally protected.

To Whom Was the Wrongdoing Reported?

The answer to this question may determine whether the potential whistleblower is a protected whistleblower. If the report was made to an "incorrect" party, it will prevent the potential whistleblower from being protected. If the report was made to a "correct" party, then the potential whistleblower may or may not be protected, depending upon other factors. Below are the more common situations that can prevent the disclosure from being protected because it was reported to the wrong individual or organization.

Disclosure to the Wrongdoer

Disclosure to the wrongdoer is typically unprotected. The MSPB's reviewing court, the Federal Circuit, has held that "[c]riticism directed to the wrongdoers themselves is not normally viewable as whistleblowing."[61] Even if the potential whistleblower makes a report to the employee's own supervisor, if the supervisor is the wrongdoer, there is no protected disclosure.[62]

The reason for this result is the meaning of the word "disclosure." In *Huffman v. Office of Personnel Management*, the Federal Circuit held that disclosure "means to reveal something that was hidden and not known."[63] As a result, if the "employee reports or states that there has been misconduct by a wrongdoer to the wrongdoer, the employee is not making a 'disclosure' of misconduct. If the misconduct occurred, the wrongdoer necessarily knew of the conduct already because he is the one that engaged in the misconduct."[64] In other words, the employee has to tell someone something they did not already know.[65]

The Federal Circuit held that it was "quite significant that Congress in the WPA" chose to use the word disclose rather than the word "report" or "state."[66] As with so much else in the law, slight differences in wording can determine the entire result. Here, the difference between "disclosure" and "report" makes the difference in whether an employee who communicates the problem to the wrongdoer will or will not be protected. Congress chose to use the word "disclosure" when drafting the WPA, and the employee's conveyance of the information is therefore unprotected if the listener was the wrongdoer.

The Federal Circuit has addressed in dictum the possibility of situations where the wrongdoing supervisor may be unaware that his or her actions are wrong.[67] The court stated that if the supervisor was aware of the *conduct*, then notifying the supervisor of the *improper nature* of the conduct would not be a protected disclosure.[68] Thus, the employee who wants to help his or her supervisor by informing the unaware supervisor of the improper nature of the conduct lacks whistleblower protection if retaliation results, even if the employee is revealing a *nature* that had been hidden from, or unknown to, the wrongdoer. Just as there is a distinction between a disclosure and a report, there is a distinction between disclosing conduct and disclosing the nature of the conduct. Potential whistleblowers should be aware of the implications of communicating a problem to the wrongdoer, even when the wrongdoer may not be aware that a problem exists, as it can make the difference in being protected or unprotected from retaliation.

Prohibited by Law or Executive Order

If, in the course of making a report of wrongdoing, the potential whistleblower makes a disclosure that is specifically ordered by law or Executive Order to be kept secret in the interest of national defense or the conduct of foreign affairs, then the disclosure is "prohibited by law" and the report of wrongdoing will not be protected unless it is to the agency's Inspector General, to "another employee designated by the head of the agency to receive such disclosures" or to the Office of the Special Counsel.[69] If the disclosure is not subject to such a prohibition, then the disclosure is not limited to these three parties and reports to other recipients, such as the media, may be protected. This makes the meaning of "prohibited by law" rather important.

In 1993, in *Kent v. General Services Administration*, the Board held that the term "law" as used in 5 U.S.C. § 2302(b)(8) "was not intended to encompass rules or regulations."[70] Before the Board modified *Kent* in its *MacLean v. Department of Homeland Security* decision, the *Kent* decision meant that an individual who disclosed information when the disclosure was prohibited only by rules or regulations, but not directly by a statute, could still obtain whistleblower protection.[71] In 2009, the Board modified its 1993 *Kent* decision by eliminating its bright line distinction between a disclosure prohibited by law and a disclosure prohibited by regulation.

In *MacLean*, the Board held that a regulation can prohibit a disclosure under section 2302(b)(8), provided that: (1) the regulation is a substantive rule; (2) Congress granted the agency authority to create such a regulation; and (3) the regulation is promulgated in a manner that meets any procedural requirements imposed by Congress.[72] A "substantive rule" is one that affects individual rights and obligations.[73] When these three conditions are met by the *regulation* requiring non-disclosure, the case will be treated as if the *law* had prohibited the disclosure.[74] However, as noted above, the Board only modified *Kent* in *MacLean* —it did not overrule *Kent.*[75] Thus, some regulations are to be given the force of law, and some are not.

The *MacLean* decision means that, in some cases, the disclosure is protected only if it is made to the agency's Inspector General, to another employee designated by the head of the agency to receive such disclosures, or to the Office of the Special Counsel. In other cases, however, a disclosure to a different party, such as the media, would still be protected. The employee might not know which category applies—and therefore to whom a protected disclosure may be made—at the time that the disclosure seems important to make. It is important for potential whistleblowers to be aware of the implications of the *MacLean* decision when deciding who to contact with a disclosure of wrongdoing that could possibly involve national security secrets. As *MacLean* demonstrated, making the disclosure to some entities versus others can carry a greater risk that the disclosure may not be protected.

Normal Course of Duties and Normal Channels

Not all disclosures are protected. A protected disclosure may fall into one of two categories: (1) disclosures as part of normal duties *outside of normal channels*; or (2) disclosures *outside of assigned duties*. If it is the regular duty of the employee to make the disclosure in question, and the disclosure is made through the usual channels employed in the performance of those duties, then the disclosure is not protected.[76]

Normal Duties and Other Employer-Assigned Obligations

With regard to the issue of normal duties, the Federal Circuit has admitted that its "jurisprudence on the normal duties question has not always been clear, and it is possible to find conflicting statements in dictum concerning the normal duties issue."[77]

In Huffman, in the hopes of clarifying the situation, the court offered three different situations, and assessed each in turn.

1) The employee has, as part of his or her normal duties, been assigned the task of investigating and reporting wrongdoing by government employees and, in fact, reports that wrongdoing through normal channels. (These are typically unprotected.)
2) The employee has been assigned such investigatory responsibilities, but feels that the normal chain of command is unresponsive, and therefore reports the wrongdoing outside of normal channels. (These can be protected disclosures.)
3) The employee is obligated to report the wrongdoing, but such a report is not part of the employee's normal duties or the employee has not been assigned those duties. (These can be protected disclosures.)[78]

The first situation—where reporting is an assigned task—will often arise in situations involving law enforcement or inspectors general. The court has held repeatedly that an employee "cannot be said to have risked his personal job security by merely performing his required duties."[79] If an employee is carrying out his or her "everyday job responsibilities" and makes the disclosure through normal channels, then the employee's disclosure is not considered protected.[80]

In order to qualify as "normal channels," the channels do not have to be formal or of a long duration. An *ad hoc* channel created by the agency to address a specific situation will qualify as the normal channel for related assignments.[81] Likewise, the duties do not have to be specifically assigned in detail.[82] In *Fields v. Department of Justice*, the Federal Circuit addressed a case in which the appellant was a Supervisory Criminal Investigator who was asked to create a timeline of events related to an investigation into his subordinate. The appellant alleged he had been retaliated against for the content of a "follow-up" memo that he considered separate from the instruction to create a timeline, and that he therefore believed "he was not required to write."[83] The court held:

> It is part of Fields's "normal duties" to participate in internal investigations when necessary, and the ad hoc reporting channels set up during an internal audit become the "normal channels" of Fields's employment for those purposes. It makes no difference that Keefe [a high ranking official] did not specifically direct Fields to prepare the second memorandum. An employee is expected to complete fully the tasks assigned to him, and in many cases that requires the employee to perform follow-up work, including the drafting of memoranda to correct mistakes, supplement the record, clarify ambiguities, and the like. Thus, we hold that when an

> employee voluntarily performs follow-up work in further response to an explicitly assigned task, that follow-up work is considered "normal duties through normal channels" and disclosures related to that follow-up work are not disclosures protected under the WPA.[84]

The second situation described in *Huffman* involves assigned duties in the same manner as the first situation, but the channel for the disclosure is different. Unlike the first situation, the second situation is "clearly a disclosure protected by the" WPA.[85] Why the different result? Making a disclosure outside of channels on the employee's own initiative in the interest of the public good makes the employee eligible for protection under the WPA.[86]

A good example of the second *Huffman* situation arose in *Johnson v. Department of Health and Human Services*. In *Johnson*, the appellant had the obligation under his assigned duties to report suspected contract irregularities. Johnson "made numerous complaints to his supervisors" regarding alleged wrongdoing, but, when he believed his concerns were being ignored, he shared his information with the Inspector General.[87] The Board held that this was the type of disclosure intended by the second situation described in *Huffman*, and was therefore protected.[88]

The Supreme Court has recognized the difficulties created by a rule that says in-house communications are unprotected, while discussions outside of normal channels may be protected. The Court advised in dictum that "[g]iving employees an internal forum for their speech will discourage them from concluding that the safest avenue of expression is to state their views in public."[89] However, for those employees who do not have a safe avenue for expression within channels, going outside channels will unfortunately be the means that affords them the best hope for protection. Once the disclosure is in the course of the employee's duties, the employee's only protection lies in ensuring it does not occur through normal channels.

The third situation occurs when there is an obligation to make a report, but it is not specifically an assigned duty. This situation can arise when there is an agency policy ordering specific conduct. For example, DEA policy requires "agents to report conduct on the part of DEA employees that either violates the agency's code of conduct or may jeopardize the mission of the agency and/or the safety of its personnel."[90] A DEA agent, Marano, made such a report about two supervisors in his Field Office. This report triggered an investigation, which in turn resulted in Marano's reassignment. The court held that Marano was a protected whistleblower.[91]

The *Marano* case points out a very fine distinction. If there is an assigned duty to make a report, and ordinary channels are used, the disclosure is not protected under the WPA. However, if there is a more general responsibility to make the report, it may be protected.[92] Because reports in the course of duties can be unprotected, this distinction is likely necessary for the WPA ever to be able to apply to a Federal employee who does not use extraordinary channels. After all, by regulation, it is a "basic obligation" of all Federal employees to "disclose waste, fraud, abuse, and corruption to appropriate authorities."[93] Thus, if a general obligation to make a disclosure were considered enough to remove protection, then no employee would be protected when disclosing fraud, waste, abuse, or corruption to "appropriate authorities."

The Professional Duty to Disclose

While the duties of a position are typically assigned by an agency, certain professions can carry a duty to disclose separate from any instructions from an employer. The issue of a public servant blowing the whistle as a part of his or her professional responsibilities was recently discussed by the Supreme Court in *Garcetti v. Ceballos*. While this case involved a county government—not the Federal Government—its holding is pertinent for all public employees. A public service employee with a professional obligation to make a disclosure will not be protected against retaliation unless there is a specific law providing protection for the particular circumstances.[94]

Ceballos was a prosecutor, employed by the county, who as a part of his assigned duties was responsible for preparing a memorandum regarding a pending case. The memorandum was critical of the activities of the county police in this particular case. Ceballos later claimed that he was retaliated against by his employer because his memorandum had spoken negatively about the police's activities. The Supreme Court held that "when public employees make statements pursuant to their official duties... the Constitution does not insulate their communications from employer discipline."[95]

In some professions—such as attorneys—there are professional requirements that could require the individual to speak (or remain silent) despite what the employer might instruct. As Justice Breyer noted in his *Garcetti* dissent, the speech of an attorney "is subject to independent regulation by canons of the profession. Those canons provide an obligation to speak in certain instances."[96] Doctors and other professionals could likewise find themselves with a professional obligation to speak up that could run counter to the instructions of a supervisor.[97] In these professions, the failure to speak can lead to a loss of the professional license, which can be a failure to maintain a condition of employment, which can be grounds to remove a Federal employee.

The Supreme Court held that withholding protection from public employees such as Ceballos was a necessary element of "affording government employers sufficient discretion to manage their operations. Employers have heightened interests in controlling speech made by an employee in his or her professional capacity. Official communications have official consequences..."[98] The Court expressed concern that to hold otherwise would mean "mandating judicial oversight" of the communications between employees and their supervisors throughout all local, state, and Federal government agencies.[99]

The Board has addressed *Garcetti* only once thus far. In 2006, a Federal employee, Chambers (discussed in the previous section on dangers to public safety), alleged in a petition for review that her disclosures regarding police coverage on the BW Parkway were protected by the First Amendment. After Chambers filed her petition for review, but before the Board issued a decision, *Garcetti* was issued. In its 2006 *Chambers* decision, the Board held that under *Garcetti*, Chambers' speech could not be protected because her "statements were made pursuant to the appellant's official duties[.]"[100] The Board also held that even under pre-*Garcetti* case law the First Amendment would not have protected Chambers because "the agency had an overriding interest in not having the Chief of the Park Police publicly question decisions made by officials who outranked her concerning the functions and budget of the Park Police."[101] The Federal Circuit later overruled the Board and found that Chambers' disclosure could be protected—but the basis for this decision was the WPA, not the First Amendment.[102] Thus, it is important to recognize that the protections available to a potential whistleblower will typically come only from the specific whistleblower laws enacted by Congress.[103] Whatever the statute does not actively protect, will generally be unprotected. And, because the Board's jurisdiction is not plenary, but is limited to those matters over which it has been granted jurisdiction,[104] the Board in particular will be unable to assist the potential whistleblower if the situation is not addressed in the law.

The Reasonable Belief

In order to be protected, the potential whistleblower does not have to be *correct* that he or she has reported wrongdoing. However, the potential whistleblower does have to *reasonably believe* the accusation revealed wrongdoing. Reporting something that the whistleblower knows is untrue is not protected.[105] An unreasonable belief is also unprotected.[106]

The test for determining whether an employee had a reasonable belief that his or her disclosures revealed wrongdoing is: "could a disinterested observer with knowledge of the essential facts known to and readily ascertainable by the employee reasonably conclude that the actions of the government evidence" wrongdoing as defined in 5 U.S.C. § 2302(b) (8)? [107] "A purely subjective perspective of an employee is not sufficient even if shared by other employees."[108]

A "determination of whether an employee has a reasonable belief that a law, rule, or regulation was violated turns on the facts of the particular case."[109] This means that the individual—who is likely not disinterested—must try to imagine what a disinterested person in his or her shoes would think about the situation. As stated before, even if other employees also share the employee's belief that there was wrongdoing, it may not be enough to prove reasonableness. Rather, the MSPB and its reviewing court will ask, what would the disinterested observer think?[110]

In order to find there was a reasonable belief, the facts on which the belief is based "must be supported by substantial evidence."[111] Substantial evidence is defined as "such relevant evidence as a reasonable mind might accept as adequate to support a conclusion."[112] Thus, the law once again brings us back to a reasonable person standard. The adjudicator will also consider any contradictory evidence, because "the substantiality of evidence must take into account whatever in the record fairly detracts from its weight."[113]

However, as stated above, the Board will reach a decision based upon *the essential facts known to and readily ascertainable by the employee.* The employee does not have to be correct in his or her analysis of those facts. For example, in *Special Counsel v. Spears*, an employee disclosed to the Inspector General that money was being spent to send two people from Missouri to training in Virginia, even though the same course was going to be offered locally in Missouri two weeks later.[114] The Inspector General later found that there was a very time-sensitive need for this training, and that it was therefore not improper to send the employees to Virginia. However, when it came to protecting the disclosure, the Board noted that the "protected status of a disclosure depends, not on whether it in fact discloses wrongdoing covered by the statute, but on whether a reasonable person would believe that what it reports is evidence of such wrongdoing." The Board held that there was "no basis for concluding that anyone who was aware of the facts about the training trip asserted in the letter would necessarily have also been aware of the time sensitive aspect" of the training. Therefore, the inaccuracy of the conclusion that the trip was improper was not relevant to the issue of whether the disclosure could be protected. It was sufficient that the facts known to the employee could cause a reasonable person to reach that conclusion.[115]

Perceived Disclosures

The Federal Circuit and the Board have repeatedly stated that one requirement for finding whistleblower retaliation is that a protected disclosure must be made.[116] However, there is an exception to this requirement. The Board has held "that the protections provided in 5 U.S.C. § 2302(b)(8) apply where a retaliatory personnel action is taken against an employee *believed* to have engaged in protected activity even though the employee may not have *actually* done so."[117]

For example, in *Thompson v. Farm Credit Administration*, the Board held that while "the appellant's expression of his view may not of itself have been intended as a disclosure of waste, fraud or abuse,"[118] the Chairman of the agency nevertheless viewed the employee "as a dangerous proponent of a view that could prove embarrassing— possibly evidencing mismanagement and abuse of discretion."[119] The Chairman also made a statement that the employee should be fired shortly after learning that the employee had distributed to other managers a study that reached conclusions that differed from the Chairman's public position.[120] Because the agency *perceived* the employee as a whistleblower, and retaliated on that basis, the employee was entitled to protection under the WPA.[121]

An Act Other Than Disclosing Wrongdoing May be Protected, but Not Necessarily as Whistleblowing

Retaliation against an employee for an employee's action is not whistleblower retaliation unless the act of the employee is to disclose a violation of any law, rule, or regulation; gross mismanagement; a gross waste of funds; an abuse of authority; or a substantial and specific danger to public health or safety. These are the criteria set forth in 5 U.S.C. § 2302(b)(8), and these are the only criteria that constitute whistleblowing under the WPA. Other retaliation, while improper, is not whistleblowing retaliation under the WPA.[122]

For example, section 2302(b)(9) is the section of the law that states that it is a prohibited personnel practice to:

> Take or fail to take, or threaten to take or fail to take, any personnel action against any employee or applicant for employment because of—
>
> (A) the exercise of any appeal, complaint, or grievance right granted by any law, rule, or regulation;
> (B) testifying for or otherwise lawfully assisting any individual in the exercise of any right referred to in subparagraph (A);
> (C) cooperating with or disclosing information to the Inspector General of an agency, or the Special Counsel, in accordance with applicable provisions of law; or
> (D) for refusing to obey an order that would require the individual to violate a law[.]

The Federal Circuit has held that these four types of behavior are *not* whistleblowing, and therefore are not protected from retaliation under the WPA. Rather, retaliation for one of the section 2302(b)(9) categories of employee action is a separate type of prohibited personnel practice.[123] This is particularly relevant in the context of Title VII offenses—situations in which an individual may believe he or she is being retaliated against for reporting a discriminatory event.

The Federal Circuit has held that in the "ongoing battle to eradicate discrimination" the "leadership role" belongs to the Equal Employment Opportunity Commission (EEOC), and reports related to such discrimination are not whistleblowing.[124] It is not that the law ignores retaliation for a report of discrimination; it is only that the protections occur outside of the whistleblower protection system. But once again, the complexities of the law put a burden on the potential whistleblower—in this case the burden to know where to go to seek redress.

RETALIATION DEFINED

Not every form of unpleasantness imposed on a Federal employee as a consequence of whistleblowing is unlawful, and therefore redressable under the whistleblower protection laws. Unlawful retaliation occurs when an "employee who has authority to take, direct others to take, recommend, or approve any personnel action" proceeds to "take or fail to take, or threaten to take or fail to take, a personnel action with respect to any employee or applicant for employment because of " the disclosure of the wrongdoing.[125]

As the Federal Circuit has put it, to establish that there has been "retaliation for whistleblowing activity, an employee must show both that she engaged in whistleblowing activity by making a disclosure protected under 5 U.S.C. § 2302(b)(8) and that the protected disclosure was a contributing factor in a personnel action."[126] Without both of these pieces, there can be no case. Thus, the potential whistleblower must not only meet the definitions of disclosure discussed in the previous chapter, but the individual must also show the agency took, or failed to take (or threatened to take or fail to take), a personnel action because of the disclosure.[127]

A Personnel Action

"A personnel action" is defined by section 2302(a)(2)(A). Under the statute, any of the following can qualify as a personnel action.

1) An appointment;
2) A promotion;
3) An action under chapter 75 of Title 5 or other disciplinary or corrective action;
4) A detail, transfer, or reassignment;
5) A reinstatement;
6) A restoration;
7) A reemployment;
8) A performance evaluation under chapter 43 of Title 5;
9) A decision concerning pay, benefits, or awards, or concerning education or training if the education or training may reasonably be expected to lead to an appointment, promotion, performance evaluation, or other action described in this subparagraph;
10) A decision to order psychiatric testing or examination;[128] and
11) Any other significant change in duties, responsibilities, or working conditions.

The third item on this list, disciplinary or corrective actions, applies to more than just actions recorded in an employee's official personnel file (OPF) such as suspensions or removals. For example, in *Johnson v. Department of Health and Human Services*, the employee received a letter of admonishment for contacting the Inspector General. The letter was not made a part of the employee's official record, and was therefore not a *disciplinary* action. However, because it was intended to modify the employee's behavior in the future (cause him to not contact the Inspector General again), it was a *corrective* action and therefore was a covered personnel action for purposes of the WPA.[129]

The ninth item on the list of potential personnel actions can encompass a frequent yet seemingly minor area of management decisions. Placing an employee in a leave without pay (LWOP) or absent without leave (AWOL) status is a decision concerning pay or benefits, and therefore is a personnel action.[130] A denial of annual leave also is a decision concerning benefits under section 2302(a)(2)(A).[131] The denial of an opportunity "to earn overtime pay that an employee would otherwise have been provided is clearly a decision concerning pay" and therefore is a personnel action.[132] Thus, when dealing with an employee who has reported wrongdoing, even seemingly minor decisions may qualify as a "personnel action" under the WPA.

The last item on the list, "any other significant change in duties, responsibilities, or working conditions" has been read to include a variety of management actions, including retaliatory investigations.

> [If] an investigation is so closely related to the personnel action that it could have been a pretext for gathering evidence to retaliate, and the agency does not show by clear and convincing evidence that the evidence would have been gathered absent the protected disclosure, then the appellant will prevail on his affirmative defense of retaliation for whistleblowing. That the investigation itself is conducted in a fair and impartial manner, or that certain acts of misconduct are discovered during the investigation, does not relieve an agency of its obligation to demonstrate by clear and convincing evidence that it would have taken the same personnel action in the absence of the protected disclosure... To here hold otherwise would sanction the use of a purely retaliatory tool, selective investigations.[133]

Examples of other retaliatory actions include the suspension of law enforcement authority for a Special Deputy U.S. Marshal and the decision not to extend an employee's overseas tour.[134]

However, there is one crucial area in which the courts have decided that an action by the agency is not a personnel action under the whistleblower protection statutes: the revocation of a security clearance.[135] The Federal Circuit has specifically held that the decision by an agency to revoke a security clearance—even when that clearance is a required condition of employment—

will not be subject to review by OSC or adjudication by the MSPB.[136] The Supreme Court has held that (in the absence of a law stating otherwise) it is "not reasonably possible" for a body such as the MSPB to review the substance of security clearance decisions and determine what constitutes an acceptable margin of error in assessing the potential risk.[137] The Federal Circuit recognizes that this leaves "federal employees without recourse to the Board or the Special Counsel if they believe they have been denied security clearances in retaliation for whistleblowing."[138]

Take or Fail to Take (or Threaten to Take or Fail to Take)

It is usually much easier to determine if a personnel action has been taken than it is to determine if an agency has failed to take a personnel action. For example, an appointment is the first item on the list of personnel actions covered by the statute.[139] If a person who has blown the whistle in the past applies for a position, but the agency cancels the vacancy announcement and never fills the position, has there been a failure to take a personnel action? According to the Federal Circuit, this can be a failure to take an action and can qualify as whistleblower reprisal if all the other conditions for whistleblowing are met.[140]

Similarly, even if the action—or inaction—never reaches fruition, there can still be whistleblower reprisal because it is retaliation just to *threaten* to take or not take a personnel action. One example of this is a Performance Improvement Plan (PIP). While a PIP is ostensibly given to an employee to aid the employee to improve his or her performance, it is also a necessary step to taking a performance based action such as a reduction in grade or a removal under 5 U.S.C. § 4301 *et seq.*[141] As such, "a PIP by definition involves a threatened personnel action" and can be the basis of a whistleblower reprisal action if all other elements of whistleblowing and reprisal are present.[142] However, the organization still has the responsibility to manage all its employees effectively—including those who may be whistleblowers. This responsibility includes taking action related to an employee's performance and conduct—provided that the employee's whistleblowing is not a contributing factor in the decision to take or not to take a particular action.

Contributing Factor

For an agency's personnel action, inaction, or threat to constitute reprisal, the whistleblowing must be a contributing factor in the agency's decision to take, not take, threaten to take, or threaten not to take the personnel action.[143] "The words a contributing factor... mean *any factor which, alone or in connection with other factors, tends to affect in any way the outcome of the decision.*"[144] Although it is very difficult to know what happens inside any person's mind, and those who retaliate will rarely document that a retaliatory motive factored into a decision, it is possible to prove through circumstantial evidence that a disclosure was a contributing factor in the taking or failure to take a personnel action.

There are two basic ways in which a potential whistleblower can establish that a disclosure was a contributing factor: (1) through the use of the knowledge/timing test; or (2) through the use of any other evidence demonstrating that the disclosure was a contributing factor. These two approaches are described below.

Knowledge/Timing Test

To establish under the knowledge/timing test that the disclosure was a contributing factor in the decision to take a personnel action, the whistleblower only needs to show "that the deciding official knew of the disclosure and that the adverse action was initiated within a reasonable time of that disclosure[.]"[145]

A "reasonable time" is not defined in the statute or regulation. However, the MSPB has found periods of more than a year between the disclosure and the personnel action sufficient to establish the connection.[146] The test used by the Federal Circuit appears to be whether or not the time "gap between the disclosures and the allegedly retaliatory action is too long an interval to justify an inference of cause and effect between the two[.]"[147]

If the knowledge/timing test is met, the "whistleblower need not demonstrate the existence of a retaliatory motive on the part of the employee taking the alleged prohibited personnel action in order to establish that [the] disclosure was a contributing factor to the personnel action[.]"[148] In fact, "[o]nce the knowledge/timing test has been met, an administrative judge *must* find that the appellant has shown that his whistleblowing was a contributing factor in the personnel action at issue, even if, after a complete analysis of all of the evidence, a reasonable factfinder could *not* conclude that the appellant's whistleblowing was a contributing factor in the personnel action."[149]

However, as discussed later in this chapter, establishing that the whistleblowing was a contributing factor does not guarantee that the employee will obtain the relief sought.

Other Evidence of a Contributing Factor

While the knowledge/timing test is the most employed method, it is not the only means by which an employee may show that a disclosure was a contributing factor.[150] If an employee cannot satisfy the knowledge/timing test, the adjudicator will consider other evidence, such as "the strength or weakness of the agency's reasons for taking the personnel action, whether the whistleblowing was personally directed at the proposing or deciding officials, and whether these individuals had a desire or motive to retaliate against the appellant."[151] It is possible to meet the contributing factor standard by combining the weight of multiple different factors.[152]

Clear and Convincing Evidence

The law states that a corrective action "may not be ordered if the agency demonstrates by *clear and convincing evidence* that it would have taken the same personnel action in the absence of " the whistleblowing.[153] "Clear and convincing evidence is that measure or degree of proof that produces in the mind of the trier of fact a firm belief as to the allegations sought to be established. It is a higher standard than preponderance of the evidence[.]"[154]

When determining whether an agency has shown by clear and convincing evidence that it would have taken the same personnel action in the absence of whistleblowing, the MSPB considers three factors: (1) whether the agency had legitimate reasons for the personnel action; (2) the existence and strength of any motive to retaliate on the part of the agency officials who were involved in the decision to take the personnel action; and (3) any evidence that the agency takes similar personnel actions against employees who are not whistleblowers but who are otherwise similarly situated.[155] These three factors have been referred to as the *Carr* factors.

One example of the application of the *Carr* factors is *Phillips v. Department of Transportation*, in which the Board concluded the agency would still have taken the same action in the absence of the protected disclosure. In *Phillips*, the appellant supervised five employees, all of whom contacted the Office of the Inspector General (OIG) to express concerns about the appellant's activities. After the OIG investigation began, the appellant was temporarily put on a telecommuting detail to an office in another state. Following this, the appellant made a disclosure that was protected under the

WPA. Several months later, the investigation was completed, and the OIG concluded that the appellant had used her public office for the gain of a private business and had violated the Standards of Ethical Conduct by maintaining a personal friendship with a principal of a carrier over which the appellant was exercising the agency's regulatory authority. Several months after the report of the investigation was issued, the appellant was reassigned from a supervisory position in Montana to a non-supervisory position at the same grade in Illinois.[156]

In assessing the first factor (any legitimate reasons for the action), the Board noted that the appellant's conduct had caused such concern for her subordinates that five employees had contacted the OIG to report it, and that "the five complainants comprised the entire Montana Division staff."[157] The Board held that "[u]nder these circumstances, the agency was legitimately concerned about returning the appellant to duty in that office, where she would be required to supervise and manage all of these complainants on a daily basis."[158]

Furthermore, since the agency had sufficient concerns that it temporarily reassigned the appellant during the investigation, before the protected disclosure, their concerns were not a mere pretext.[159]

When assessing the second factor (any motive for retaliation), the Board noted that one of the officials involved in the decision to reassign the appellant had a strong motive to retaliate because he was a chief subject of the appellant's disclosure. However, another official's motive was unclear, and the two officials most involved in the decision lacked a strong motive to retaliate.[160]

Lastly, for the third factor (personnel actions for similarly situated individuals), the appellant claimed that employees who committed similar offenses had not been subjected to similar personnel actions, but the Board held that the other employees were not similarly situated because they did not have close social relationships with carriers they regulated, and there was no indication of the problems with the other staff in the office such as was present in the appellant's case.[161]

Accordingly, the Board held that under the *Carr* factors, the agency had met its burden to show, by clear and convincing evidence, that it would have taken the same personnel action in the absence of the whistleblowing.[162]

AVENUES FOR REDRESS

There are three means by which a whistleblower case may come before the Merit Systems Protection Board: (1) from a complaint filed by the OSC under the Board's original jurisdiction; (2) from an individual right of action (IRA) appeal filed by a person alleging retaliation; or (3) from an individual's appeal of an otherwise appealable action (OAA). In the absence of such jurisdiction, the MSPB lacks the authority to consider the case.

Original Jurisdiction

An original jurisdiction whistleblower protection case comes before the MSPB when the Office of the Special Counsel concludes that an agency has likely retaliated against an employee on the basis of the employee's protected disclosure of wrongdoing and OSC seeks to correct the agency's action.[163] However, before such a case can come before the MSPB, OSC must notify the agency involved that OSC has determined that there are reasonable grounds to believe that the prohibited personnel practice of whistleblower retaliation has occurred. It is only if the agency fails to correct the retaliation "after a reasonable period of time" that OSC would then petition the MSPB for corrective action.[164] The law also permits OSC to bring a case to the MSPB based upon the commission of other PPPs. According to the OSC, "[t]ypically, OSC obtains corrective action through negotiation between the complainant and the agency."[165] Thus, corrective action cases against an agency are rarely brought to the MSPB under its original jurisdiction for the commission of *any* prohibited personnel practice.

From January 1, 1995 to December 31, 2009, OSC filed only 32 corrective action cases related to PPPs, and of those cases, 16 were settled after the complaint was filed with the MSPB. More common are requests from OSC for MSPB to order an agency to stay a personnel action while OSC investigates the potential that the action involves a prohibited personnel action (such as whistleblower retaliation), or while OSC pursues a settlement agreement.[166]

When OSC files an original jurisdiction corrective action case with the MSPB, OSC must present a complaint and the supporting facts to both the employee and the MSPB.[167] The agency involved, OSC, and the Office of Personnel Management (OPM) are entitled to make oral or written comments.[168] While the OSC corrective action statute does not specify that a hearing must be conducted, MSPB regulations state that a corrective action complaint will be assigned to a judge for a hearing.[169]

Once OSC's complaint is received by the MSPB, an administrative law judge (ALJ) is assigned to hear the complaint. The ALJ will conduct a hearing, consider the evidence and issue an initial decision.[170] The decision of the ALJ is subject to review by the three-member Board of the MSPB. That decision, in turn, is subject to review on appeal to the Federal Circuit. While the impacted employee does not prosecute the case before the MSPB in an original jurisdiction case, the employee may appeal the outcome to the Federal Circuit if the employee is "adversely affected or aggrieved" by the MSPB's final order or decision.[171]

Individual Right of Action (IRA) Appeal

In 1989, Congress was concerned that "OSC had not brought a single corrective action case since 1979 to the Merit Systems Protection Board on behalf of a whistleblower."[172] In order to strengthen protections for whistleblowers the Whistleblower Protection Act of 1989 granted to potential whistleblowers an individual right of action to pursue their own cases before the MSPB, rather than relying on OSC to prosecute the case.[173] An IRA appeal occurs under the MSPB's appellate jurisdiction, but it carries important conditions to establish jurisdiction that a more traditional appeal does not require.

In an IRA appeal, an appellant must first establish that MSPB has jurisdiction by making non-frivolous allegations that: (1) the appellant engaged in whistleblowing activity by making a protected disclosure under 5 U.S.C. § 2302(b)(8); (2) based on the protected disclosure, the agency took or failed to take a personnel action (or made such a threat); (3) the appellant sought corrective action from OSC; and (4) the appellant exhausted corrective action proceedings before OSC.[174] The elements of a protected disclosure and the connection to a personnel action are required for any whistleblower case. The last two elements are unique to IRA appeals, and they can cause significant difficulties for IRA appellants.[175]

Before the MSPB can adjudicate an IRA appeal, the individual must try to get OSC to take a corrective action. By law, the MSPB lacks the authority to adjudicate any claim until a statute has given the MSPB jurisdiction.[176] For an IRA appeal, MSPB's jurisdiction is triggered "[o]nly after OSC has notified the employee that it has terminated its investigation or has failed to commit to pursuing corrective action within 120 days[.]"[177] If there was never a complaint filed with OSC, then MSPB cannot have jurisdiction over an IRA appeal.[178]

When an individual files an IRA appeal with the MSPB, it is crucial that the issues raised in the IRA be the same as those contained in the individual's earlier complaint to OSC. "The purpose of the requirement that an employee exhaust his or her remedies before the Special Counsel before appealing to the Board is to give the Special Counsel the opportunity to take corrective action before involving the Board in the case."[179] This means that the appellant must provide enough detail to OSC that there is a "sufficient basis to pursue an investigation which might have led to corrective action."[180] "The test of the sufficiency of an employee's charges of whistleblowing to the OSC is the statement that the employee makes in the complaint [to OSC]... not the employee's post hoc characterization of those statements."[181] If the appellant has not provided the necessary "clarity and precision" in the OSC complaint, then the appellant will have "deprived the Board of jurisdiction to hear his appeal for corrective action."[182] In other words, if it was not in the original complaint, it cannot be adjudicated in the IRA action.[183]

For this reason, it is crucial that any potential whistleblower who seeks protection from a retaliatory personnel action treat the OSC complaint process very seriously, and not as a mere formality. While there have been extensive discussions amongst stakeholders about why OSC brings so few corrective actions for whistleblowing, the reality is that the process for seeking a corrective action is important beyond OSC's decision on whether to proceed. Even if the OSC does not prosecute the complaint before the MSPB, the potential whistleblower should treat it very seriously and ensure the complaint contains important details. Failure to do so can prevent the MSPB from having jurisdiction over the IRA appeal.

Once an individual has completed the required steps above, the individual may file an IRA appeal with the MSPB. Such an appeal is filed with one of the MSPB's field or regional offices. The case is then assigned to an administrative judge (AJ). If the AJ determines there is reason to believe that the MSPB may have jurisdiction, the AJ will conduct any hearing, consider the evidence, and issue an initial decision.[184] That decision may be appealed to the three-member Board of the MSPB on a petition for review (PFR). An employee also may appeal either the initial decision, or the PFR decision, to the Federal Circuit.

Otherwise Appealable Actions Jurisdiction

Most Federal employees have the right to appeal certain personnel actions to the MSPB, separate from any implications of whistleblower retaliation.[185] In a traditional adverse action appeal, the appellant has the burden to prove any affirmative defense by a preponderance of the evidence.[186]

The personnel actions that may be appealed under the MSPB's adverse action appellate jurisdiction include, but are not limited to, removals, reductions in grade or pay, suspensions of more than 14 days, and furloughs of 30 days or less.[187] If an employee who has adverse action appeal rights believes that the adverse action was taken in retaliation for the individual's whistleblowing, then the employee may use the MSPB's traditional appellate jurisdiction and raise whistleblower retaliation as an affirmative defense. *A separate complaint to OSC is not required if the individual was affected by a personnel action that is directly appealable to the MSPB.* Furthermore, an employee is permitted to exercise his or her adverse action appeal rights, even if he or she has filed a complaint with OSC, provided that the employee also follows all of the adverse action appeal procedures, and the MSPB has not adjudicated the content of the OSC complaint on the merits.[188]

Because retaliation against a whistleblower is one of the PPPs, if the employee can demonstrate in a traditional appeal that the action qualifies as whistleblower retaliation, and the agency cannot show by clear and convincing evidence that it would have taken the same action in the absence of the whistleblowing, the MSPB will overturn the agency's action.[189] The employee will be restored to the *status quo ante* (the same situation that he or she was in prior to the unwarranted adverse personnel action.)[190]

MSPB Jurisdiction over Non-Whistleblowing Retaliation Claims

As discussed earlier, section 2302(b)(9) applies when an agency official retaliates against an employee because the employee filed a complaint, grievance, or appeal; testified in such a case; cooperated with certain investigations; or refused to violate the law. Such retaliation by an agency is not automatically whistleblower retaliation, but it is nonetheless a prohibited personnel practice. Because OSC has jurisdiction over all prohibited personnel practices, OSC has the power to bring a section 2302(b)(9) case to the attention of the MSPB. The MSPB is specifically authorized (and even instructed) by statute to "order such corrective action as the Board considers appropriate, if the Board determines that the Special Counsel has demonstrated that a prohibited personnel practice, other than one described in section 2302(b)(8), has occurred, exists, or is to be taken."[191] Thus, a section 2302(b)(9) PPP action may come before the MSPB as a part of its original jurisdiction.

Because an agency official's desire to punish an employee for exercising an appeal right, cooperating with an investigation, or refusing to violate the law, is not a legitimate reason to take an adverse personnel action, a section 2302(b)(9) PPP could also come to the attention of the MSPB as a part of an employee's affirmative defense in an traditional appealable action.[192]

However, the MSPB will not have jurisdiction over a purely section 2302(b)(9) PPP if it comes to the MSPB in the form of an IRA appeal. The logic behind this is the fact that IRA appeals are reserved for *whistleblowers*, and someone who is retaliated against under section 2302(b)(9) is subjected to a non-whistleblower PPP.

The Federal Circuit has held that when establishing the IRA avenue for redress, Congress "drew a distinction between reprisal based on disclosure of information and reprisal based upon exercising a right to complain."[193] "The facts underlying a section 2302(b)(9) disclosure can serve as the basis for a section 2302(b)(8) disclosure only if they establish the type of fraud, waste, or abuse that the WPA was intended to reach."[194] Without this connection to whistleblowing, the MSPB simply lacks the legal authority to hear the claim under its whistleblower retaliation adjudication authority.[195] This is one more reason why it is important for an employee to make use of the Office of the Special Counsel. OSC can obtain from the MSPB the necessary corrective action for any PPP (including a section 2302(b)(9) PPP) while the individual acting alone cannot overcome the jurisdictional hurdle in the absence of some other appeal right.

CONCLUSION

Whistleblower protection is a particularly complex area of Federal personnel law. As we discussed in this report, the MSPB will not be able to provide relief under the WPA to a Federal employee or applicant who discloses wrongdoing and believes that he or she has been retaliated against for the disclosure, unless all of the following conditions are met:

1) The individual disclosed conduct that meets a specific category of wrongdoing set forth in the law.
2) The individual made the disclosure to the "right" type of party. Depending on the nature of the disclosure, the individual may be limited regarding to whom the report can be made.
3) The individual made a report that is either: (a) outside of the employee's course of duties; or (b) communicated outside of normal channels.
4) The individual made the report to someone other than the wrongdoer.
5) The individual had a reasonable belief of wrongdoing.
6) The individual suffered a personnel action, the agency's failure to take a personnel action, or the threat to take or not take a personnel action.
7) The individual was able to demonstrate a connection between the disclosure and the personnel action, failure to take a personnel action, or the threat to take or not take a personnel action.
8) The individual sought redress through the proper channels.

However, even if an individual establishes all of the above criteria are met, the law states that the relief sought by the individual will not be ordered if the agency can establish by clear and convincing evidence that it would have taken the same action in the absence of the whistleblowing.

This means that not all undesirable conduct by an agency constitutes wrongdoing, not all reports of wrongdoing constitute disclosures, and not all disclosures are protected. Furthermore, not all unpleasantness for the whistleblower that results from whistleblowing constitutes a prohibited personnel practice for which a legal remedy may be obtained. Lastly, if there has been whistleblower retaliation, certain procedural steps often must be followed by the whistleblower in order to obtain redress.

If the employee's situation is not one covered by the statutes, the MSPB will lack the authority to reach the merits of a potential whistleblower's appeal. That is why it is so important for Federal employees to understand how the whistleblower protections work and for Congress to be aware of the difficulties a potential whistleblower may encounter when navigating the law.

It is not surprising that Congress has seen the need to amend whistleblower laws in the past, and has considered doing so again in recent years. It is challenging to create a set of rules that carefully balances management rights with the public's interest in protecting whistleblowers. A perfect balance between management rights and whistleblower protections may never be fully achieved, but we believe that the best possible balance is worth pursuing. As the Senate noted when the CSRA was enacted, and whistleblower protections were put into the law for Federal employees for the first time: "Protecting employees who disclose government illegality, waste, and corruption is a major step toward a more effective civil service."[196]

EXCERPTS FROM TITLE 5

The below are excerpts from the law, provided to aid in the discussion throughout this report. Please consult the full text of any statute when using the law for any other purpose.

Definition of Personnel Action

§ 2302 (a)(2) For the purpose of this section—

(A) "personnel action" means—

I. an appointment;
II. an promotion;
III. an action under chapter 75 of this title or other disciplinary or corrective action;
IV. a detail, transfer, or reassignment;
V. a reinstatement;
VI. a restoration;
VII. a reemployment;
VIII. a performance evaluation under chapter 43 of this title;
IX. a decision concerning pay, benefits, or awards, concerning education or training if the education or training may reasonably be expected to lead to an appointment, promotion, performance evaluation, or other action described in this subparagraph;
X. a decision to order psychiatric testing or examination; and
XI. any other significant change in duties, responsibilities, or working conditions;

with respect to an employee in, or applicant for, a covered position in an agency, and in the case of an alleged prohibited personnel practice described in subsection (b)(8), an employee or applicant for employment in a Government corporation as defined in section 9101 of title 31...

Whistleblower Retaliation Provision

§ 2302 (b) Any employee who has authority to take, direct others to take, recommend, or approve any personnel action, shall not, with respect to such authority—

(8) take or fail to take, or threaten to take or fail to take, a personnel action with respect to any employee or applicant for employment because of—

(A) any disclosure of information by an employee or applicant which the employee or applicant reasonably believes evidences—

(i) a violation of any law, rule, or regulation, or

(ii) gross mismanagement, a gross waste of funds, an abuse of authority, or a substantial and specific danger to public health or safety,

if such disclosure is not specifically prohibited by law and if such information is not specifically required by Executive order to be kept secret in the interest of national defense or the conduct of foreign affairs; or

(B) any disclosure to the Special Counsel, or to the Inspector General of an agency or another employee designated by the head of the agency to receive such disclosures, of information which the employee or applicant reasonably believes evidences—

(i) a violation of any law, rule, or regulation, or

(ii) gross mismanagement, a gross waste of funds, an abuse of authority, or a substantial and specific danger to public health or safety...

Retaliation That Is a PPP, but Is Not Whistleblower Retaliation

§ 2302 (b) Any employee who has authority to take, direct others to take, recommend, or approve any personnel action, shall not, with respect to such authority—

(9) take or fail to take, or threaten to take or fail to take, any personnel action against any employee or applicant for employment because of—

A. the exercise of any appeal, complaint, or grievance right granted by any law, rule, or regulation;

B. testifying for or otherwise lawfully assisting any individual in the exercise of any right referred to in subparagraph (A);
C. cooperating with or disclosing information to the Inspector General of an agency, or the Special Counsel, in accordance with applicable provisions of law; or
D. for refusing to obey an order that would require the individual to violate a law...

Individual Right of Action (IRA)

§ 1214 (a)(3) ... An employee, former employee, or applicant for employment may seek corrective action from the Board under section 1221, if such employee, former employee, or applicant seeks corrective action for a prohibited personnel practice described in section 2302 (b)(8) from the Special Counsel and—

(A)

(i) the Special Counsel notifies such employee, former employee, or applicant that an investigation concerning such employee, former employee, or applicant has been terminated; and

(ii) no more than 60 days have elapsed since notification was provided to such employee, former employee, or applicant for employment that such investigation was terminated; or

(B)

120 days after seeking corrective action from the Special Counsel, such employee, former employee, or applicant has not been notified by the Special Counsel that the Special Counsel shall seek corrective action on behalf of such employee, former employee, or applicant.

§ 1221(e)(1) Subject to the provisions of paragraph (2), in any case involving an alleged prohibited personnel practice as described under section 2303 (b)(8), the Board shall order such corrective action as the Board considers appropriate if the employee, former employee, or applicant for employment has demonstrated that a disclosure described under section 2303 (b)(8) was a contributing factor in the personnel action which was taken or is to be taken against such employee, former employee, or applicant. The employee may demonstrate that the disclosure was a contributing factor in the personnel action through circumstantial evidence, such as evidence that—

(A) the official taking the personnel action knew of the disclosure; and

(B) the personnel action occurred within a period of time such that a reasonable person could conclude that the disclosure was a contributing factor in the personnel action.

(2) Corrective action under paragraph (1) may not be ordered if the agency demonstrates by clear and convincing evidence that it would have taken the same personnel action in the absence of such disclosure.

End Notes

[1] 5 U.S.C. § 2302(b)(8).

[2] It is the practice of the U.S. Merit Systems Protection Board to refer to the agency as a whole as "the MSPB" and the 3-member board that issues precedential decisions as "the Board." We have therefore used this language in this report. However, when other authorities (such as statutes or the Federal Circuit) refer to this agency, the agency as a whole is often called "the Board." Thus, some quotations within this report refer to "the Board" when discussing the powers or responsibilities of the agency, while outside of quotations, the term "the Board" is reserved for the 3-member body that issues our precedential decisions.

[3] 5 U.S.C. § 1204(a)(3).

[4] The MSPB has previously issued reports specifically about whistleblowing in 1981 and 1993, as well as addressing whistleblowing in various other reports and newsletter articles. For a full list of whistleblower-related studies and articles, please visit our website at www.mspb.gov/studies.

[5] An intangible effect, such as having co-workers no longer be as friendly towards the employee is not a personnel action. Certain other types of actions—particularly the revocation of a security clearance—are also not personnel actions that can be challenged under whistleblower protection laws, even though the loss of a security clearance could lead to the loss of Federal employment.

[6] Unless the personnel action is one for which the MSPB has a separate jurisdictional authority, the employee first must seek redress through the Office of the Special Counsel (OSC). Failure to present OSC with a detailed complaint and to wait for OSC to conclude its investigation (or wait 120 days if the investigation is not concluded), will prevent the MSPB from obtaining jurisdiction to hear the claim.

[7] 5 U.S.C. § 1221(e)(2). Clear and convincing evidence is that measure or degree of proof that produces in the mind of the trier of fact a firm belief as to the allegations sought to be established. It is a higher standard of proof than preponderance of the evidence. 5 C.F.R. § 1209.4(d).

[8] S. Rep. 95-969, 8 (1978 U.S.C.C.A.N. 2723, 2730). (This is the Senate Report that accompanied the Civil Service Reform Act of 1978.)

[9] The whistleblower protection laws apply to applicants for employment in addition to current Federal employees. 5 U.S.C. § 2302(a)(2)(A). However, because most whistleblowing

retaliation claims involve employees, in the interest of simplicity, this report will not make repeated references to applicants.

[10] The Board is specifically prohibited, by statute, from providing any advisory opinions. 5 U.S.C. § 1204(h).

[11] 5 U.S.C. § 2302(b)(8).

[12] Committee on Governmental Affairs, *The Whistleblowers: A Report on Federal Employees Who Disclose Acts of Governmental Waste, Abuse, and Corruption*, February, 1978, p. 4. (Senator Leahy's report was published by the Committee as a service to the public with a note that the Committee took "no position" on its content.)

[13] S. Rep. 95-969, 8 (1978 U.S.C.C.A.N. 2723, 2730).

[14] S. Rep. 95-969, 24 (1978 U.S.C.C.A.N. 2723, 2746).

[15] S. Rep. 103-358, 2 (1994 U.S.C.C.A.N. 3549, 3550).

[16] An affirmative defense occurs when an employee claims that an action should not be sustained because: (1) there was a harmful error in the agency's procedures for taking the action; (2) the decision was based on a PPP (such as whistleblower retaliation); or (3) the decision was otherwise not in accordance with the law. 5 U.S.C. § 7701(c)(2). While an agency has the burden to prove its action is supported by a preponderance of the evidence, the appellant asserting an affirmative defense bears the burden to prove the affirmative defense by a preponderance of the evidence. 5 C.F.R. § 1201.56(a)(2).

[17] The 1994 amendments to the WPA were intended to clarify the rules governing OSC disclosure of information about whistleblowers; require OSC to provide appropriate information to whistleblowers whose cases have been closed; establish a fixed time limit for OSC to take action on whistleblower cases; and ensure that whistleblowers have access to relevant evidence in the event that they bring their own cases to the MSPB. S. Rep. 103-358, 1-2 (1994 U.S.C.C.A.N. 3549, 3550).

[18] Cases where jurisdiction is shared by both the MSPB and the Equal Employment Opportunity Commission (mixed cases) are appealable to the Federal district courts, and from there, to the geographically-based circuit courts rather than the Federal Circuit.

[19] "Under 5 U.S.C. § 7703(b)(1), as amended, the United States Court of Appeals for the Federal Circuit has exclusive jurisdiction over petitions for judicial review of Board decisions with respect to cases other than those involving claims of prohibited discrimination. Given this exclusive grant of jurisdiction, the Board has held that decisions by that court are controlling authority on the Board, whereas decisions by other circuit courts are persuasive, but not controlling, authority." *Fairall v. Veterans Administration,* 33 M.S.P.R. 33, 39 (1987), *aff'd,* 844 F.2d 775 (Fed. Cir. 1987).

[20] U.S. Court of Appeals for the Federal Circuit, Rule 32.1(d)).

[21] Unlike the Federal Circuit, where a party from a case has a right of appeal, the Supreme Court has sole discretion to decide if it will hear an MSPB case from the Federal Circuit. This is called granting or denying *certiorari*, or "*cert.*" Throughout the footnotes in this report, some case references will say "*cert. denied.*" This means that a party requested a review by the Supreme Court, and the Supreme Court declined to hear the case. While a few cases heard before the MSPB have been granted *certiorari*, it is very rare. Deliberate changes to a statute to prevent the Federal Circuit's analysis from applying to future cases have also occurred, but are rare. Typically, the decision of the Federal Circuit is the final word.

[22] Unlike the definition of an employee for purposes of appealing an adverse action— which excludes most probationers and most temporary employees—the term "employee" has a broad definition for whistleblowing, and probationers are potentially protected, as are temporary employees and applicants for employment. *Horton v. Department of the Navy*, 66

F.3d 279, 282 (Fed. Cir. 1995); *Lopez v. Department of Housing and Urban Development*, 98 F.3d 1358 (Fed. Cir. 1996) (Table); 5 U.S.C. § 2302(a)(2)(A). For more information regarding when a probationer or temporary employee has an appeal right for a non-whistleblower adverse action, please see our report *Navigating the Probationary Period After Van Wersch and McCormick*, available at www.mspb.gov/studies.

[23] 5 U.S.C. § 2302(b)(8)(A).

[24] *Langer v. Department of the Treasury*, 265 F.3d 1259, 1266 (Fed. Cir. 2001).

[25] *Drake v. Agency for International Development*, 543 F.3d 1377, 1381 (Fed. Cir. 2008). In *Drake*, the court noted that cases in which violations were considered trivial focused on "inadvertent" behavior, while non-trivial violations tended to be "deliberate and intentional" behavior. *See Langer v. Department of the Treasury*, 265 F.3d 1259, 1267 (Fed. Cir. 2001); *Herman v. Department of Justice*, 193 F.3d 1375, 1381 (Fed. Cir. 1999) (holding that the reported behavior was inadvertent and thus the report was not a covered disclosure). *But see Horton v. Department of the Navy*, 66 F.3d 279, 283 (Fed. Cir. 1995) (holding that disclosing a seemingly minor event can be a qualified disclosure when its purpose is to show the existence of a repeated practice).

[26] *Lawley v. Department of the Treasury*, 84 M.S.P.R. 253, 18 (1999).

[27] *Wojcicki v. Department of the Air Force*, 72 M.S.P.R. 628, 635 (1996).

[28] *Grubb v. Department of the Interior*, 96 M.S.P.R. 377, 25- 28 (2004).

[29] *Drake v. Agency for International Development*, 543 F.3d 1377, 1380-81 (Fed. Cir. 2008).

[30] *Mogyorossy v. Department of the Air Force*, 96 M.S.P.R. 652, 11 (2004). *See also Ganski v. Department of the Interior,* 86 M.S.P.R. 32, 11 (2000).

[31] *Daniels v. Department of Veterans Affairs*, 105 M.S.P.R. 248, 12 (2007) (holding that the appellant's "allegations appear to so obviously implicate a violation of law, rule, or regulation that she need not have identified any specific law, rule, or regulation that was violated"); *Kalil v. Department of Agriculture*, 96 M.S.P.R. 77, 16 (2004) (holding that although the appellant did not cite any specific law, rule, or regulation, his disclosure could reasonably be regarded as evidencing a violation of an obstruction of justice statute); *Ivey v. Department of the Treasury,* 94 M.S.P.R. 224, 13 (2003) (holding that although the appellant did not cite any specific law, rule, or regulation that his disclosures violated, his disclosure relating to the alteration of tax returns could reasonably be regarded as violating regulatory, if not statutory, provisions).

[32] *DiGiorgio v. Department of the Navy*, 84 M.S.P.R. 6, 14 (1999).

[33] "Abuse of authority does not incorporate a *de minimis* standard." *Embree v. Department of the Treasury*, 70 M.S.P.R. 79, 85 (1996).

[34] This definition was created by the Office of the Special Counsel prior to the WPA of 1989. The definition no longer exists in regulations, but because it existed at the time of the 1989 WPA, and Congress opted in 1989 not to provide a different meaning, the Board determined it was appropriate to use this definition for abuse of authority. *D'Elia v. Department of the Treasury*, 60 M.S.P.R. 226, 232 (1993). *See also Elkassir v. General Services Administration*, 257 Fed. Appx. 326, 329 (Fed. Cir. 2007) (Table); *Doyle v. Department of Veterans Affairs*, 273 Fed. Appx. 961 (Fed. Cir. 2008) (Table); *Gilbert v. Department of Commerce*, 194 F.3d 1332 (Fed. Cir. 1999) (Table).

[35] *D'Elia v. Department of the Treasury*, 60 M.S.P.R. 226, 232 (1993).

[36] *Special Counsel v. Costello,* 75 M.S.P.R. 562, 580-81 (1997) *rev'd on other grounds,* 182 F.3d 1372 (Fed. Cir. 1999); *Murphy v. Department of the Treasury*, 86 M.S.P.R. 131, 7 (2000).

[37] *Loyd v. Department of the Treasury*, 69 M.S.P.R. 684, 688 (1996).

[38] *Sirgo v. Department of Justice*, 66 M.S.P.R. 261, 267 (1995). *But see Special Counsel v. Spears*, 75 M.S.P.R. 639, 655 (1997) (holding that a perception of "favoritism" in work assignment decisions does not constitute a reasonable belief in improper preferential treatment of an employee unless there is also a prohibited purpose behind the making of those assignments.)

[39] *Wheeler v. Department of Veterans Affairs*, 88 M.S.P.R. 236, 13 (2001).

[40] *Pulcini v. Social Security Administration*, 83 M.S.P.R. 685, 13 (1999).

[41] *McCollum v. Department of Veterans Affairs*, 75 M.S.P.R. 449, 458-59 (1997) (holding that the employee failed to show that his rights were adversely affected by the issuance of a new performance appraisal plan or a progress review, or that these actions resulted in personal gain or advantage to another).

[42] *Downing v. Department of Labor*, 98 M.S.P.R. 64, 12 (2004) (holding that there was no allegation that particular individuals' rights were affected or that the office closure was for personal gain).

[43] *Schneider v. Department of Homeland Security*, 98 M.S.P.R. 377, 13 (2005). *See also* 5 U.S.C. § 2302(b)(8).

[44] *McCorcle v. Department of Agriculture*, 98 M.S.P.R. 363, 22 (2005); *Lopez v. Department of Housing and Urban Development*, 98 F.3d 1358 (Fed. Cir. 1996) (Table); *White v. Department of the Air Force*, 391 F.3d 1377, 1382 (Fed. Cir. 2004); *Czarkowski v. Department of the Navy*, 87 M.S.P.R. 107, 12 (2000) (holding that gross mismanagement "is a decision that creates a substantial risk of significant adverse impact upon the agency's ability to accomplish its mission.")

[45] *Sazinski v. Department of Housing and Urban Development*, 73 M.S.P.R. 682, 686-87 (1997); *McCorcle v. Department of Agriculture*, 98 M.S.P.R. 363, 22 (2005); *White v. Department of the Air Force*, 391 F.3d 1377, 1384 (Fed. Cir. 2004) (holding that "[b]ecause a disinterested observer with knowledge of all the essential facts known to and readily ascertainable by White at the time of his disclosure would have concluded that the merits of the... program that White criticized were debatable by reasonable people, White could not have a reasonable belief that he disclosed gross mismanagement.")

[46] *Lopez v. Department of Housing and Urban Development*, 98 F.3d 1358 (Fed. Cir. 1996) (Table) (quoting *Nafus v. Department of the Army*, 57 M.S.P.R. 386, 395 (1993)).

[47] *White v. Department of the Air Force*, 391 F.3d 1377, 1382 (Fed. Cir. 2004).

[48] *Wood v. Department of Defense*, 100 M.S.P.R. 133, 12 (2005).

[49] *Swanson v. General Services Administration*, 110 M.S.P.R. 278, 11 (2008).

[50] *Sazinski v. Department of Housing and Urban Development*, 73 M.S.P.R. 682, 687 (1997) (holding that the "appellant could not have reasonably believed that the elimination of 'several' positions from an engineering staff 'down somewhat' from 80 [previous engineers] would have a substantial adverse impact on the agency's ability to accomplish its mission.") *See also McCorcle v. Department of Agriculture*, 98 M.S.P.R. 363, 22 (2005) (holding that a disclosure by an employee that he believed his talents were underutilized was not "sufficient to indicate that he reasonably believed" that decisions regarding his assignments "would have a substantial adverse impact on the agency's ability to accomplish its mission.")

[51] *Jensen v. Department of Agriculture*, 104 M.S.P.R. 379, 10 (2007) (citing *Van Ee v. Environmental Protection Agency*, 64 M.S.P.R. 693, 698 (1994)).

[52] *Jensen v. Department of Agriculture*, 104 M.S.P.R. 379, 9 (2007).

[53] *Smith v. Department of the Army*, 80 M.S.P.R. 311, 6, 10 (1998).

[54] *Parikh v. Department of Veterans Affairs*, 110 M.S.P.R. 295, 18 (2008).

[55] *Chambers v. Department of the Interior*, 515 F.3d 1362, 1369 (Fed. Cir. 2008). The *Chambers* case has an extensive history. As of July 2010 there have been two Board decisions and two Federal Circuit decisions. At the time this report was written, *Chambers* was before the Board on its second remand from the Federal Circuit.

[56] *Chambers v. Department of the Interior*, 602 F.3d 1370, 1379 (Fed. Cir. 2010).

[57] *Miller v. Department of Homeland Security*, 111 M.S.P.R. 312, 16-19 (2009).

[58] *Mogyorossy v. Department of the Air Force*, 96 M.S.P.R. 652, 16-17 (2004).

[59] *See Braga v. Department of the Army*, 54 M.S.P.R. 392, 398 (1992), *aff'd,* 6 F.3d 787 (Fed. Cir. 1993) (holding that the complaint of a designer of body armor for soldiers that the specifications he was told to meet could leave the soldiers in danger of being maimed or killed constituted a protected disclosure of a danger to public safety); *Gady v. Department of the Navy*, 38 M.S.P.R. 118, 121 (1988) (holding that a report of a fire hazard and threat to the health of the agency's staff could be a protected disclosure).

[60] *Wojcicki v. Department of the Air Force*, 72 M.S.P.R. 628, 634-35 (1996). *See also Braga v. Department of the Army,* 54 M.S.P.R. 392, 398 (1992), *aff'd,* 6 F.3d 787 (Fed. Cir. 1993).

[61] *Horton v. Department of the Navy*, 66 F.3d 279, 282 (Fed. Cir. 1995).

[62] *Huffman v. Office of Personnel Management*, 263 F.3d 1341, 1350 (Fed. Cir. 2001).

[63] *Huffman v. Office of Personnel Management*, 263 F.3d 1341, 1349-50 (Fed. Cir. 2001).

[64] *Huffman v. Office of Personnel Management*, 263 F.3d 1341, 1350 (Fed. Cir. 2001).

[65] In *Meuwissen v. Department of the Interior*, 234 F.3d 9, 13 (Fed. Cir. 2000), the Federal Circuit held that the "disclosure of information that is publicly known is not a disclosure under the WPA. The purpose of the WPA is to protect employees who possess knowledge of wrongdoing that is concealed or not publicly known, and who step forward to help uncover and disclose that information." However, if an employee adds "additional information necessary to recognize" the nature or seriousness of the problem, and this is information the general public would not have, then a disclosure may be protected, even if the more factual part of the disclosure could be observed by the public. *Wadhwa v. Department of Veterans Affairs*, 110 M.S.P.R. 615, 9 (2009).

[66] *Huffman v. Office of Personnel Management*, 263 F.3d 1341, 1350 (Fed. Cir. 2001).

[67] Dictum (or dicta) refers to a comment by the court that is not considered necessary to the result in the case, and therefore is not binding. However, the comment has the effect of letting the reader know how the court might possibly view the issue in a future case.

[68] *Huffman v. Office of Personnel Management*, 263 F.3d 1341, 1350 n. 2 (Fed. Cir. 2001). ("To be sure, there may be situations where a government employee reports to the wrongdoer that the conduct of the wrongdoer is unlawful or improper, and the wrongdoer, though aware of the conduct, was unaware that it was unlawful or improper. Nonetheless, the report would not be a protected disclosure. It is clear from the statute, 5 U.S.C. § 2302(b)(8)(A), that the disclosure must pertain to the underlying conduct, rather than to the asserted fact of its unlawfulness or impropriety, in order for the disclosure to be protected by the WPA.")

[69] 5 U.S.C. § 2302(b)(8).

[70] *Kent v. General Services Administration*, 56 M.S.P.R. 536, 542 (1993).

[71] *Kent v. General Services Administration*, 56 M.S.P.R. 536, 542 (1993).

[72] *MacLean v. Department of Homeland Security*, 112 M.S.P.R. 4, 25 (2009) (citing *Chrysler Corp. v. Brown*, 441 U.S. 281, 301-03 (1979)).

[73] *MacLean v. Department of Homeland Security*, 112 M.S.P.R. 4, 26 (2009) (citing *Chrysler Corp. v. Brown*, 441 U.S. 281, 302 (1979)). In *Chrysler*, the regulations in question were found to "certainly affect individual rights and obligations" because they governed the public's right to information in records obtained under an Executive Order and the

confidentiality rights of those who submit information to the Government. *Chrysler Corp. v. Brown*, 441 U.S. 281, 303 (1979).

[74] *MacLean v. Department of Homeland Security*, 112 M.S.P.R. 4, 26 (2009) (citing *Chrysler Corp. v. Brown*, 441 U.S. 281, 302 (1979)).

[75] The specific language used by the Board was: "to the extent that *Kent v. General Services Administration* holds that a regulation could never be a law prohibiting disclosure within the meaning of 5 U.S.C. § 2302(b)(8)(A), we modify it." *MacLean v. Department of Homeland Security*, 112 M.S.P.R. 4, 33 n. 2 (2009) (internal citation deleted).

[76] *Fields v. Department of Justice*, 452 F.3d 1297, 1305 (Fed. Cir. 2006) (citing *Huffman v. Office of Personnel Management*, 263 F.3d 1341, 1354 (Fed. Cir. 2001)).

[77] *Huffman v. Office of Personnel Management*, 263 F.3d 1341, 1351-52 (Fed. Cir. 2001).

[78] *Huffman v. Office of Personnel Management*, 263 F.3d 1341, 1352-54 (Fed. Cir. 2001) (holding that "[a] report may be a disclosure protected by the Act, though the employee can also be disciplined for failure to make the report.")

[79] *Willis v. Department of Agriculture*, 141 F.3d 1139, 1144 (Fed. Cir. 1998). *See also Huffman v. Office of Personnel Management*, 263 F.3d 1341, 1351-52 (Fed. Cir. 2001).

[80] *Willis v. Department of Agriculture*, 141 F.3d 1139, 1144 (Fed. Cir. 1998). *See also Laberge v. Department of the Navy*, 91 M.S.P.R. 585, 8 (2002) (holding that a disclosure by the appellant expressing concern that environmental statutes and regulations were not being followed was unprotected because "he was investigating and reporting wrongdoing as part of his normal duties through normal channels.")

[81] *Fields v. Department of Justice*, 452 F.3d 1297, 1305 (Fed. Cir. 2006).

[82] *Fields v. Department of Justice*, 452 F.3d 1297, 1305 (Fed. Cir. 2006). *See also Layton v. Department of the Army*, 112 M.S.P.R. 549, 15 (2009) (holding that a disclosure was not protected because although the disclosure was not a part of the appellant's usual duties, the expansion of his duties was with the express authorization of supervisors who provided oversight of—and input into—the product that ultimately constituted the employee's disclosure.)

[83] *Fields v. Department of Justice*, 452 F.3d 1297, 1305 (Fed. Cir. 2006).

[84] *Fields v. Department of Justice*, 452 F.3d 1297, 1305 (Fed. Cir. 2006).

[85] *Huffman v. Office of Personnel Management*, 263 F.3d 1341, 1354 (Fed. Cir. 2001).

[86] It is possible for an employee to make a disclosure both through normal channels, and outside those channels. Provided that one of the channels used for a disclosure provides protection under the WPA, the use of additional channels will not negate that protection. That disclosures to different parties "stem from the same set of operative facts is not necessarily inconsistent with the Board's jurisdiction" over an appeal. *Ellison v. Merit Systems Protection Board*, 7 F.3d 1031, 1035 (Fed. Cir. 1993). *See also Martin v. Department of the Air Force*, 73 M.S.P.R. 574, 578-79 (1997) (holding that just because an "appellant repeated his allegations in other forums, does not affect the fact that he made disclosures outside the other forums.")

[87] In *Johnson*, the Board noted that in *Huffman*, the Federal Circuit "did not state or suggest that there was any requirement of an objective showing that a reasonable person would have believed it was necessary" to go outside of the normal channels. Thus, while it must be reasonable for a person to suspect the alleged wrongdoing, it appears that the decision to go outside of the normal channels is not subject to the reasonable person standard. *Johnson v. Department of Health and Human Services*, 93 M.S.P.R. 38, 13-14 (2002).

[88] *Johnson v. Department of Health and Human Services*, 93 M.S.P.R. 38, 14 (2002).

[89] *Garcetti v. Ceballos*, 547 U.S. 410, 424 (2006).

[90] *Marano v. Department of Justice*, 2 F.3d 1137, 1142 n.4 (Fed. Cir. 1993). *See also Watson v. Department of Justice*, 64 F.3d 1524, 1530 (Fed. Cir. 1995) (an employee was removed for, among other things, violating agency regulations by not timely reporting misconduct by a coworker by the end of his duty shift.) In *Huffman*, *Watson* was specifically cited by the Federal Circuit as an example of a situation where there was an obligation to disclose, and yet the disclosure could be protected (although Watson's removal was upheld for other reasons.) *Huffman v. Office of Personnel Management*, 263 F.3d 1341, 1354 (Fed. Cir. 2001).

[91] *Marano v. Department of Justice*, 2 F.3d 1137 (Fed. Cir. 1993).

[92] *See Kahn v. Department of Justice*, 528 F.3d 1336, 1342-43 (Fed. Cir. 2008) (holding that while a disclosure of wrongdoing was required of all DEA agents, the disclosure could be protected when it was not part of the employee's normal duties.)

[93] 5 C.F.R. § 2635.101(b)(11).

[94] *Garcetti v. Ceballos*, 547 U.S. 410 (2006). In *Garcetti*, the employee sought protection under the First Amendment to the U.S. Constitution, likely because there was no law that provided him protection based upon his professional obligations.

[95] *Garcetti v. Ceballos*, 547 U.S. 410, 421 (2006).

[96] *Garcetti v. Ceballos*, 547 U.S. 410, 446 (2006) (Breyer, J. dissenting).

[97] *Garcetti v. Ceballos*, 547 U.S. 410, 447 (2006) (Breyer, J. dissenting).

[98] *Garcetti v. Ceballos*, 547 U.S. 410, 422 (2006).

[99] *Garcetti v. Ceballos*, 547 U.S. 410, 423 (2006).

[100] *Chambers v. Department of the Interior*, 103 M.S.P.R. 375, 35 (2006) *overruled on other grounds by Chambers v. Department of the Interior*, 515 F.3d 1362 (Fed. Cir. 2008).

[101] *Chambers v. Department of the Interior*, 103 M.S.P.R. 375, 40 (2006) *overruled on other grounds by Chambers v. Department of the Interior*, 515 F.3d 1362 (Fed. Cir. 2008).

[102] *Chambers v. Department of the Interior*, 602 F.3d 1370, 1379 (Fed. Cir. 2010).

[103] There are some laws to protect Federal employees outside the whistleblower context that can also be used to protect an employee who happens to be a whistleblower, such as the appeal rights provided to an employee who is suspended for more than 14 days, changed to a lower grade, or removed. *See Massimino v. Department of Veterans Affairs*, 58 M.S.P.R. 318, 322-24 (1993).

[104] *Stoyanov v. Department of the Navy*, 474 F.3d 1377, 1379 (Fed. Cir. 2007) (citing *Clark v. Merit Systems Protection Board,* 361 F.3d 647, 650 (Fed. Cir. 2004)).

[105] *Thompson v. Department of the Treasury*, 155 F.3d 574 (Fed. Cir. 1998) (Table). *See also* S. Rep. 95-969, 22 (1978 U.S.C.C.A.N. 2723, 2744) (stating that "an employee should not be protected... for making a disclosure which he knows to be false.")

[106] *Lachance v. White,* 174 F.3d 1378, 1381 (Fed. Cir. 1999), *cert. denied,* 528 U.S. 1153, 120 (2000).

[107] *Lachance v. White,* 174 F.3d 1378, 1381 (Fed. Cir. 1999), *cert. denied,* 528 U.S. 1153, 120 (2000).

[108] *Lachance v. White,* 174 F.3d 1378, 1381 (Fed. Cir. 1999), *cert. denied,* 528 U.S. 1153, 120 (2000).

[109] *Herman v. Department of Justice,* 193 F.3d 1375, 1382 (Fed. Cir. 1999).

[110] *Lachance v. White,* 174 F.3d 1378, 1381 (Fed. Cir. 1999), *cert. denied,* 528 U.S. 1153, 120 (2000).

[111] *Frederick v. Department of Justice*, 73 F.3d 349, 352 (Fed. Cir. 1996).

[112] *Frederick v. Department of Justice*, 73 F.3d 349, 352 (Fed. Cir. 1996) (citing *Consolidated Edison Co. v. NLRB*, 305 U.S. 197, 229 (1938)).

[113] *Frederick v. Department of Justice*, 73 F.3d 349, 352 (Fed. Cir. 1996) (citing *Universal Camera Corp. v. NLRB,* 340 U.S. 474, 488 (1951)).

[114] *Special Counsel v. Spears*, 75 M.S.P.R. 639, 657 (1997).

[115] *Special Counsel v. Spears*, 75 M.S.P.R. 639, 659 (1997). *See also Baldwin v. Department of Veterans Affairs*, 113 M.S.P.R. 469, 18-21 (2010) (holding that the Board will "consider concepts of criminal law from a layman's perspective" when evaluating if a reasonable person would believe he or she was disclosing a violation of law when reporting that a co-worker allegedly threatened the employee with a box cutter.)

[116] *Warren v. Department of the Army*, 804 F.2d 654, 656 (Fed. Cir. 1986); *Drake v. Agency for International Development*, 543 F.3d 1377, 1380 (Fed. Cir. 2008); *Lachance v. White*, 174 F.3d 1378, 1380 (Fed. Cir. 1999); *Eidmann v. Merit Systems Protection Board,* 976 F.2d 1400, 1407 (Fed. Cir. 1992); *Worthington v. Department of Defense*, 81 M.S.P.R. 532, 10 (1999).

[117] *Special Counsel v. Department of the Navy*, 46 M.S.P.R. 274, 280 (1990) (emphasis added). *See also Sirgo v. Department of Justice,* 66 M.S.P.R. 261, 266 (1995); *Thompson v. Farm Credit Administration,* 51 M.S.P.R. 569, 580-81 (1991); *Juffer v. U.S. Information Agency*, 80 M.S.P.R. 81, 12 (1998); *Zimmerman v. Department of Housing and Urban Development*, 61 M.S.P.R. 75, 83 (1994).

[118] *Thompson v. Farm Credit Administration*, 51 M.S.P.R. 569, 581 (1991).

[119] *Thompson v. Farm Credit Administration*, 51 M.S.P.R. 569, 582 (1991).

[120] *Thompson v. Farm Credit Administration*, 51 M.S.P.R. 569, 581 (1991).

[121] The evidence in this particular case contained "a great deal of circumstantial evidence of retaliation." *Thompson v. Farm Credit Administration*, 51 M.S.P.R. 569, 583 (1991).

[122] It is possible that a Federal employee who reports an issue may be protected by a statute other than the WPA. For example, the Energy Reorganization Act protects individuals who disclose violations of certain statutes, and it specifically includes the Department of Energy as a covered employer. 42 U.S.C. § 5851(a)(2)(G). However, some Federal whistleblower protection statutes specifically exclude Federal employees from their protections. For example, the Occupational Safety and Health Act of 1970 will protect some whistleblowers, but the definition of the term "employer" specifically "does not include the United States... or any State or political subdivision of a State." 29 U.S.C. § 652(5). *See also* the Surface Transportation Assistance Act, which specifically defines a protected individual as a person who "is not an employee of the United States Government, a State, or a political subdivision of a State acting in the course of employment." 49 U.S.C. § 31105(j)(2).

[123] *Spruill v. Merit Systems Protection Board*, 978 F.2d 679, 690-92 (Fed. Cir. 1992). Because such retaliation would be a prohibited personnel practice under 5 U.S.C. § 2302(b)(9), redress could be sought through means other than the WPA. For example, the employee could file a grievance under a collective bargaining agreement (if eligible), a grievance under the agency's administrative grievance procedures (if eligible), or a complaint with the Office of the Special Counsel.

[124] *Spruill v. Merit Systems Protection Board*, 978 F.2d 679, 692 (Fed. Cir. 1992).

[125] 5 U.S.C. § 2302(b).

[126] *Briley v. National Archives & Records Administration*, 236 F.3d 1373, 1378 (Fed. Cir. 2001). *See also* 5 U.S.C. § 1221(e)(1); *Yunus v. Department of Veterans Affairs*, 242 F.3d 1367, 1371 (Fed. Cir. 2001); *Meuwissen v. Department of the Interior*, 234 F.3d 9, 12 (Fed. Cir. 2000).

[127] As will be discussed later, the timing between the agency's knowledge of the whistleblowing and the taking of the personnel action can be used to establish that the disclosure was a contributing factor in the decision to take the personnel action.

[128] The inclusion of a psychiatric exam as a personnel action may appear odd in comparison to the other items on the list, but it reflects the history of whistleblower retaliation. Historically, one method used to deflect attention from a potential whistleblower's charges was (and still is) to attack the credibility of the potential whistleblower and make the situation about the person doing the reporting rather than the original wrongdoing being reported. Requiring the potential whistleblower to submit to a psychiatric examination is therefore a particularly suspect activity.

[129] *Johnson v. Department of Health and Human Services*, 93 M.S.P.R. 38, 15-16 (2002) (holding "that the letter of admonishment was not a part of the appellant's official personnel records is irrelevant to the question of whether it was a covered personnel action.")

[130] *McCorcle v. Department of Agriculture*, 98 M.S.P.R. 363, 16 (2005).

[131] *Marren v. Department of Justice,* 50 M.S.P.R. 369, 373 (1991).

[132] *DiGiorgio v. Department of the Navy*, 84 M.S.P.R. 6, 18 (1999).

[133] *Russell v. Department of Justice*, 76 M.S.P.R. 317, 324-25 (1997).

[134] *Johns v. Department of Veterans Affairs*, 95 M.S.P.R. 106, 11-13 (2003); *Woodworth v. Department of the Navy*, 105 M.S.P.R. 456, 18 (2007).

[135] The Board has held that "in an adverse action over which the Board has jurisdiction and which is based substantially on the agency's revocation or denial of a security clearance, the Board has no authority to review the agency's stated reasons for the security clearance determination." *Egan v. Department of the Navy*, 28 M.S.P.R. 509, 519 (1985). (In *Egan v. Department of the Navy*, 802 F.2d 1563, 1575 (Fed. Cir. 1986), the Federal Circuit reversed this holding by the Board, but that court was in turn reversed by the Supreme Court, which supported the Board's interpretation of the law. *Department of the Navy v. Egan*, 484 U.S. 518, 526-32 (1988)).

[136] When applying the Supreme Court's *Egan* decision to the issue of whistleblowers, the Board has held, and the Federal Circuit has affirmed, that "because the [Whistleblower Protection] Act does not specifically authorize the Board to review security clearance determinations, it cannot serve as a basis for Board jurisdiction" in a WPA case. *Hesse v. Department of State,* 217 F.3d 1372, 1380 (Fed. Cir. 2000). There are also no Fifth Amendment Due Process Clause rights regarding the revocation of a security clearance. *Robinson v. Department of Homeland Security*, 498 F.3d 1361, 1364-65 (Fed. Cir. 2007).

[137] *Department of the Navy v. Egan*, 484 U.S. 518, 529 (1988).

[138] *Hesse v. Department of State*, 217 F.3d 1372, 1380 (Fed. Cir. 2000).

[139] 5 U.S.C. § 2302(a)(2)(A)(i).

[140] *Ruggieri v. Merit Systems Protection Board*, 454 F.3d 1323, 1326 (Fed. Cir. 2006).

[141] For more on performance-based actions taken under Chapter 43 of Title 5, please see our recent report, *Addressing Poor Performers and the Law*, available at www.mspb.gov/studies.

[142] *Gonzales v. Department of Housing and Urban Development*, 64 M.S.P.R. 314, 319 (1994). *See also Czarkowski v. Department of the Navy*, 87 M.S.P.R. 107, 18 (2000); *Hudson v. Department of Veterans Affairs*, 104 M.S.P.R. 283, 15 (2006).

[143] 5 U.S.C. § 1214(b)(4)(B)(i); 5 U.S.C. § 1221(e)(1). In 1993, the Federal Circuit held that circumstantial evidence of a personnel action taken soon after a protected disclosure was made was insufficient to establish a *prima facie* case of reprisal. *Clark v. Department of the Army,* 997 F.2d 1466 (Fed. Cir. 1993), *cert. denied,* 510 U.S. 1091 (1994). This decision

was expressly overruled by an Act of Congress. Public Law No. 103-424, codified at 5 U.S.C. § 1221(e)(1)(A) and (B); S. Rep. 103-358, 7 (1994 U.S.C.C.A.N. 3549, 3555) (stating that "[t]his provision reverses the holding of *Clark v. Department of Army*, decided July 1, 1993, by the U.S. Court of Appeals for the Federal Circuit.") *See also Horton v. Department of the Navy*, 66 F.3d 279, 284 (Fed. Cir. 1995).

[144] *Marano v. Department of Justice*, 2 F.3d 1137, 1140 (Fed. Cir. 1993) (internal punctuation deleted). This test was specifically intended to overrule earlier case law, which required a whistleblower to prove that his protected conduct was a significant, motivating, substantial, or predominant factor in a personnel action in order to overturn that action. *Id.*

[145] *Reid v. Merit Systems Protection Board*, 508 F.3d 674, 678-79 (Fed. Cir. 2007) (internal punctuation deleted). *See also Kewley v. Department of Health & Human Services*, 153 F.3d 1357, 1361 (Fed. Cir. 1998).

[146] *See Inman v. Department of Veterans Affairs*, 112 M.S.P.R. 280, 12 (2009) (a gap of approximately 15 months between the disclosure and the action satisfied the knowledge/timing test); *Redschlag v. Department of the Army*, 89 M.S.P.R. 589, 87 (2001) (a gap of approximately 18 months after one disclosure and more than one year after another disclosure satisfied the knowledge/timing test); *Russell v. Department of Justice*, 76 M.S.P.R. 317, 323 (1997) (a gap of 7 months satisfied the knowledge/timing test); *Easterbrook v. Department of Justice*, 85 M.S.P.R. 60, 10 (2000) (a gap of 7 months satisfied the knowledge/timing test). *But see Costello v. Merit Systems Protection Board*, 182 F.3d 1372, 1377 (Fed. Cir. 1999) (personnel action taken more than 2 years after the disclosure did not satisfy the knowledge/timing test).

[147] *Costello v. Merit Systems Protection Board*, 182 F.3d 1372, 1377 (Fed. Cir. 1999).

[148] *Kewley v. Department of Health and Human Services*, 153 F.3d 1357, 1362 (Fed. Cir. 1998) (quoting *Marano v. Department of Justice*, 2 F.3d 1137, 1141 (Fed. Cir. 1993)).

[149] *Schnell v. Department of the Army*, 114 M.S.P.R. 83, 21 (2010) (emphasis added). *See also Carey v. Department of Veterans Affairs*, 93 M.S.P.R. 676, 13 (2003).

[150] The knowledge/timing test is "only one of many possible ways that a whistleblower" can show that the whistleblowing was a factor in the personnel action. S. Rep. 103-358, 8 (1994 U.S.C.C.A.N. 3549, 3556).

[151] *Powers v. Department of the Navy*, 69 M.S.P.R. 150, 156 (1995) (internal citations deleted).

[152] *See Marano v. Department of Justice,* 2 F.3d 1137, 1140 (Fed. Cir. 1993); *Mausser v. Department of the Army,* 63 M.S.P.R. 41, 45 (1994); *Powers v. Department of the Navy*, 69 M.S.P.R. 150, 156 (1995).

[153] 5 U.S.C. § 1221(e)(2) (emphasis added).

[154] 5 C.F.R. § 1209.4 (d). *See also Horton v. Department of the Navy*, 66 F.3d 279, 284 (Fed. Cir. 1995).

[155] *Schnell v. Department of the Army*, 114 M.S.P.R. 83, 23 (2010) (citing *Carr v. Social Security Administration*, 185 F.3d 1318, 1323 (Fed. Cir. 1999)). In *Schnell v. Department of the Army*, the appellant claimed that the agency's retaliation took the form of his non-selection for a temporary promotion. In response, the agency submitted affidavits from Calvert and Neitzel [the first and second level supervisors] containing only general statements that they never took any retaliatory personnel actions against the appellant. Neither Calvert nor Neitzel, however, provided any detailed explanation as to why the agency selected other applicants over the appellant for these positions that had considerable overlap with his then current position. Nor did the agency present any other evidence of the selection procedure that it followed in filling the positions or that would explain why the appellant was not considered the top applicant for them. As a result, the agency failed to meet its burden to

create in the minds of the Board members the required "firm belief" that the action would have taken place in the absence of the whistleblowing. *Id.* 24.

[156] *Phillips v. Department of Transportation*, 113 M.S.P.R. 73, 2-6, 19 (2010).

[157] *Phillips v. Department of Transportation*, 113 M.S.P.R. 73, 19 (2010).

[158] *Phillips v. Department of Transportation*, 113 M.S.P.R. 73, 12-18 (2010).

[159] *Phillips v. Department of Transportation*, 113 M.S.P.R. 73, 20-21 (2010).

[160] *Phillips v. Department of Transportation*, 113 M.S.P.R. 73, 26-29 (2010).

[161] *Phillips v. Department of Transportation*, 113 M.S.P.R. 73, 30 (2010).

[162] *Phillips v. Department of Transportation*, 113 M.S.P.R. 73, 31 (2010).

[163] 5 U.S.C. § 1214(b)(2)(C). OSC may also seek disciplinary action against an employee who has committed whistleblower retaliation. 5 U.S.C. § 1215.

[164] 5 U.S.C. § 1214(b)(2)(B) and (C).

[165] U.S. Office of Special Counsel, *Annual Report to Congress for FY 2008*, p. 11, available at www.osc.gov. In accordance with 5 U.S.C. § 1218, data regarding OSC's investigations and settlements is publicly available in OSC's annual reports.

[166] Data on stay requests and complaints filed is from MSPB's Law Manager case docketing system.

[167] 5 C.F.R. §§ 1201.128, 1201.129.

[168] 5 U.S.C. § 1214(b)(3). OPM has a statutory right to intervene in cases before the MSPB, and to seek judicial review of any final order or decision of the MSPB, if there is the potential for an erroneous interpretation of a civil service law, rule, or regulation affecting personnel management that would have a substantial impact on such law, rule, or regulation. 5 U.S.C. § 7701(d); 5 U.S.C. § 7703(d).

[169] 5 U.S.C. § 1214(b)(3); 5 C.F.R. § 1201.131.

[170] Unlike a disciplinary action, a corrective action does not specifically require the use of an ALJ. 5 C.F.R. §§ 1201.125, 1201.131. However, it is the Board's practice to assign an ALJ to both disciplinary and corrective actions brought under the Board's original jurisdiction authority.

[171] 5 U.S.C. § 7703(a)(1).

[172] S. Rep. 103-358, 2 (1994 U.S.C.C.A.N. 3549, 3550).

[173] S. Rep. 103-358, 2 (1994 U.S.C.C.A.N. 3549, 3550).

[174] *Schmittling v. Department of the Army*, 219 F.3d 1332, 1336 (Fed. Cir. 2000). *See also Serrao v. Merit Systems Protection Board,* 95 F.3d 1569, 1574 (Fed. Cir. 1996); *Rusin v. Department of the Treasury*, 92 M.S.P.R. 298, 8 (2002).

[175] An appellant "bears the burden of showing that she sought corrective action from the OSC and that she exhausted her remedies there." *Briley v. National Archives & Records Administration*, 236 F.3d 1373, 1377 (Fed. Cir. 2001).

[176] As the Federal Circuit frequently notes in its decisions regarding MSPB, "[t]he Board's jurisdiction is not plenary, but is limited to those matters over which it has been granted jurisdiction by law, rule, or regulation." *Stoyanov v. Department of the Navy*, 474 F.3d 1377, 1379 (Fed. Cir. 2007) (citing *Clark v. Merit Systems Protection Board,* 361 F.3d 647, 650 (Fed. Cir. 2004)).

[177] *Serrao v. Merit Systems Protection Board*, 95 F.3d 1569, 1574 (Fed. Cir. 1996).

[178] While the absence of a complaint filed with OSC will cause an IRA appeal to be dismissed, premature filing is a relatively minor problem that can be overcome. If the individual files an IRA appeal without first receiving a letter from OSC stating the investigation has been terminated, or does not wait for 120 days to pass from the time the complaint was filed with OSC before filing the appeal, the IRA appeal is dismissed at the first level of the appeal (the

regional or field office administrative judge) for a lack of jurisdiction. Such dismissals are typically without prejudice, meaning that the appellant may re-file once the time period has passed (or the investigation has been closed) and the appeal has become ripe. Also, if the appellant files a petition for review (PFR) of the dismissal, and the 120 days expire while the appeal is pending with the Board, the action would then become ripe. It is the Board's practice to forward such ripened cases back to the regional or field office for adjudication. *Becker v. Department of Veterans Affairs*, 112 M.S.P.R. 516, 7 (2009).

[179] *Ward v. Merit Systems Protection Board*, 981 F.2d 521, 526 (Fed. Cir. 1992).

[180] *Ward v. Merit Systems Protection Board*, 981 F.2d 521, 526 (Fed. Cir. 1992).

[181] *Langer v. Department of the Treasury*, 265 F.3d 1259, 1268 (Fed. Cir. 2001) (internal punctuation deleted).

[182] *Ellison v. Merit Systems Protection Board*, 7 F.3d 1031, 1037 (Fed. Cir. 1993). However, it is not necessary for every conceivable detail to be included in the complaint to OSC. For example, in *Briley v. National Archives & Records Administration,* 236 F.3d 1373, 1378 (Fed. Cir. 2001), the appellant "gave a more detailed account of her whistleblowing activities" to the hearing judge than she had provided in her letters to the OSC. However, Briley's letters to the OSC nevertheless contained "the core of Briley's retaliation claim" and gave OSC a sufficient basis to pursue an investigation. They therefore satisfied Briley's "obligation to seek corrective action and exhaust her remedies before the OSC."

[183] While the individual must provide a specific and detailed allegation of wrongdoing, the MSPB does "not require, as a basis for its jurisdiction, that an appellant in an IRA appeal correctly label a category of wrongdoing under section 2302(b)(8)." *Rzucidlo v. Department of the Army*, 101 M.S.P.R. 616, 13 (2006). The focus is on whether a reasonable person could believe there was wrongdoing, not the labeling of which type of wrongdoing was disclosed. Thus, for example, if conduct is wrongly labeled by an appellant as a violation of a law, rule, or regulation when it is actually an abuse of authority, the mislabeling will not prevent the appellant from obtaining relief. "Requiring an appellant to correctly label his claim of whistleblowing is the sort of artificial distinction or technicality that led to the enactment of the WPA of 1989." *Thomas v. Department of the Treasury*, 77 M.S.P.R. 224, 236 (1998), *overruled on other grounds by Ganski v. Department of the Interior*, 86 M.S.P.R. 32 (2000).

[184] "If the employee successfully makes nonfrivolous allegations of jurisdiction, the Board then conducts a hearing on the merits." *Kahn v. Department of Justice*, 528 F.3d 1336, 1341 (Fed. Cir. 2008) (citing *Yunus v. Department of Veterans Affairs,* 242 F.3d 1367, 1371 (Fed. Cir. 2001); *Spruill v. Merit Systems Protection Board,* 978 F.2d 679, 687-88 (Fed. Cir. 1992)). A "hearing with respect to the existence of jurisdiction is unnecessary." *Id.* (citing *Francisco v. Office of Personnel Management*, 295 F.3d 1310, 1313 (Fed. Cir. 2002)).

[185] Not every individual employed by the Federal Government will meet the definition of employee for purposes of adverse action appeal rights. For example, a temporary employee who is fired for whistleblowing may file an IRA appeal, but under most circumstances, this same individual cannot be heard by the MSPB on an adverse action appeal. *See Lopez v. Department of Housing and Urban Development*, 98 F.3d 1358 (Fed. Cir. 1996) (Table). For a statutory definition of those individuals with adverse action appeal rights, *see* 5 U.S.C. § 7511(a). For a more detailed explanation regarding which individuals may have adverse action appeal rights, *see Navigating the Probationary Period After Van Wersch and McCormick*, available at www.mspb.gov/studies.

[186] 5 C.F.R. § 1201.56(a)(2)(iii). Preponderance of the evidence means "[t]he degree of relevant evidence that a reasonable person, considering the record as a whole, would accept as

sufficient to find that a contested fact is more likely to be true than untrue." 5 C.F.R. § 1201.56(c)(2).

[187] *See* 5 U.S.C. §§ 7512, 7513. While suspensions of 14 days or less are considered adverse actions, these actions cannot be appealed to the MSPB in the absence of another jurisdictional authority.

[188] *Sabersky v. Department of Justice*, 91 M.S.P.R. 210, 6-8 (2002), *aff'd*, 61 Fed.Appx. 676 (Fed. Cir. 2003); *Massimino v. Department of Veterans Affairs*, 58 M.S.P.R. 318, 324 (1993). "Generally, the Board has held that an individual who appeals his removal directly to the Board is barred by res judicata from bringing, after exhausting the OSC process, a second whistleblower appeal challenging the same removal action." *Calvetti v. Department of the Air Force*, 107 M.S.P.R. 480, 9 n. 2 (2007). If an appellant who is eligible for a traditional appeal first seeks corrective action from OSC, and then files a traditional appeal, the time limit for filing the traditional appeal is the same as it would be for an IRA appeal. *Massimino v. Department of Veterans Affairs*, 58 M.S.P.R. 318, 323 (1993). *See also* 5 C.F.R. § 1209.5(b).

[189] 5 U.S.C. § 7701(c)(2)(B); 5 U.S.C. § 1221(e)(2).

[190] "[W]hen the Board finds a personnel action unwarranted, the aim is to place the appellant, as nearly as possible, in the situation she would have been in had the wrongful personnel action not occurred." *Driscoll v. U.S. Postal Service*, 112 M.S.P.R. 498, 13 (2009). *See also Kerr v. National Endowment for the Arts*, 726 F.2d 730, 733 (Fed. Cir. 1984) (holding that an "injured party is to be placed, as near as may be, in the situation he would have occupied if the wrong had not been committed.")

[191] 5 U.S.C. §1214.

[192] An "agency's decision may not be sustained...if the employee... shows that the decision was based on any prohibited personnel practice described in section 2302(b) of this title[.]" 5 U.S.C. § 7701(c)(2)(B).

[193] *Serrao v. Merit Systems Protection Board*, 95 F.3d 1569, 1575 (Fed. Cir. 1996) (internal punctuation deleted).

[194] *Ellison v. Merit Systems Protection Board*, 7 F.3d 1031, 1035 (Fed. Cir. 1993).

[195] Because a violation of 5 U.S.C. § 2302(b)(9) is a PPP, a section 2302(b)(9) case can be adjudicated by the MSPB as an affirmative defense in an otherwise appealable action or in a PPP complaint filed by the OSC without the requirement to establish whistleblowing occurred.

[196] S. Rep. 95-969, 8 (1978 U.S.C.C.A.N. 2723, 2730).

In: Whistleblowing by Federal Employees ISBN: 978-1-63117-480-3
Editor: Bernard L. Gallagher

Chapter 3

PUBLIC LAW 112-199 (WHISTLEBLOWER PROTECTION ENHANCEMENT ACT OF 2012)*

AN ACT

To amend chapter 23 of title 5, United States Code, to clarify the disclosures of information protected from prohibited personnel practices, require a statement in non-disclosure policies, forms, and agreements that such policies, forms, and agreements conform with certain disclosure protections, provide certain authority for the Special Counsel, and for other purposes.

Be it enacted by the Senate and House of Representatives of the United States of America in Congress assembled,

Section 1. Short Title

This Act may be cited as the ''Whistleblower Protection Enhancement Act of 2012''.

---

* This is an edited, reformatted and augmented version of Public Law 112-199 dated Nov. 27, 2012.

Title I—Protection of Certain Dis- Closures of Information by Fed- Eral Employees

Sec. 101. Clarification of Disclosures Covered

(a) In General.—Section 2302(b)(8) of title 5, United States

Code, is amended—

(1) in subparagraph (A)(i), by striking ''a violation'' and inserting ''any violation''; and

(2) in subparagraph (B)(i), by striking ''a violation'' and inserting ''any violation (other than a violation of this section)''.

(b) Prohibited Personnel Practices Under Section 2302(b)(9).—

(1) Technical And Conforming Amendments.—Title 5, United States Code, is amended—

(A) in subsections (a)(3), (b)(4)(A), and (b)(4)(B)(i) of section 1214 and in subsections (a), (e)(1), and (i) of section 1221, by inserting ''or section 2302(b)(9) (A)(i), (B), (C), or (D)'' after ''section 2302(b)(8)'' each place it appears; and

(B) in section 2302(a)(2)(C)(i), by inserting ''or section 2302(b)(9) (A)(i), (B), (C), or (D)'' after ''(b)(8)''.

(2) Other References.—(A) Title 5, United States Code, is amended in subsection (b)(4)(B)(i) of section 1214 and in subsection (e)(1) of section 1221 by inserting ''or protected activity'' after ''disclosure'' each place it appears.

(B) Section 2302(b)(9) of title 5, United States Code, is amended—

(i) by striking subparagraph (A) and inserting the following:

''(A) the exercise of any appeal, complaint, or grievance right granted by any law, rule, or regulation—

''(i) with regard to remedying a violation of para- graph (8); or ''(ii) other than with regard to remedying a viola- tion of paragraph (8);''; and

(ii) in subparagraph (B), by inserting ''(i) or (ii)'' after ''subparagraph (A)''.

(C) Section 2302 of title 5, United States Code, is amended by adding at the end the following:

''(f)(1) A disclosure shall not be excluded from subsection (b)(8)

because—

''(A) the disclosure was made to a supervisor or to a person who participated in an activity that the employee or applicant reasonably believed to be covered by subsection (b)(8)(A)(i) and (ii);

''(B) the disclosure revealed information that had been pre- viously disclosed;

''(C)of the employee's or applicant's motive for making the disclosure;

''the disclosure was not made in writing;

''(E) the disclosure was made while the employee was off duty; or

''(F) of the amount of time which has passed since the occurrence of the events described in the disclosure.

''(2) If a disclosure is made during the normal course of duties of an employee, the disclosure shall not be excluded from subsection (b)(8) if any employee who has authority to take, direct others to take, recommend, or approve any personnel action with respect to the employee making the disclosure, took, failed to take, or threatened to take or fail to take a personnel action with respect to that employee in reprisal for the disclosure.''

Sec. 102. Definitional Amendments

Section 2302(a)(2) of title 5, United States Code, is amended— (1) in subparagraph (B)(ii), by striking ''and'' at the end; (2) in subparagraph (C)(iii), by striking the period at the end and inserting ''; and''; and (3) by adding at the end the following:

''(D) 'disclosure' means a formal or informal communication or transmission, but does not include a communication concerning policy decisions that lawfully exercise discretionary authority unless the employee or applicant providing the disclosure reasonably believes that the disclosure evidences—

''(i) any violation of any law, rule, or regulation; or

''(ii) gross mismanagement, a gross waste of funds, an abuse of authority, or a substantial and specific danger to public health or safety.''

Sec. 103. Rebuttable Presumption

Section 2302(b) of title 5, United States Code, is amended by amending the matter following paragraph (12) to read as follows:

''This subsection shall not be construed to authorize the withholding of information from Congress or the taking of any personnel action against an employee who discloses information to Congress. For purposes of paragraph (8), (i) any presumption relating to the performance of a duty by an employee whose conduct is the subject of a disclosure as defined under subsection (a)(2)(D) may be rebutted by substantial evidence, and (ii) a determination as to whether an employee or applicant reasonably believes that such employee or applicant has disclosed information that evidences any violation of law, rule, regulation, gross mismanagement, a gross waste of funds, an abuse of authority, or a substantial and specific danger to public health or safety shall be made by determining whether a disinterested observer with knowledge of the essential facts known to and readily ascertainable by the employee or applicant could reasonably conclude that the actions of the Government evidence such violations, mismanagement, waste, abuse, or danger.''

Sec. 104. Personnel Actions and Prohibited Personnel Prac- Tices

(a) Personnel Action.—Section 2302(a)(2)(A) of title 5, United States Code, is amended—

(1) in clause (x), by striking ''and'' after the semicolon; and

(2) by redesignating clause (xi) as clause (xii) and inserting after clause (x) the following:

''(xi) the implementation or enforcement of any non-disclosure policy, form, or agreement; and''.

(b) Prohibited Personnel Practice.—

(1) In General.—Section 2302(b) of title 5, United States Code, is amended—

(A) in paragraph (11), by striking ''or'' at the end;

(B) in paragraph (12), by striking the period and

inserting ''; or''; and

(C) by inserting after paragraph (12) the following:

''(13) implement or enforce any nondisclosure policy, form, or agreement, if such policy, form, or agreement does not contain the following statement: 'These provisions are consistent with and do not supersede, conflict with, or otherwise alter the employee obligations, rights, or liabilities created by existing statute or Executive order relating to (1) classified information, (2) communications to Congress, (3) the reporting to an Inspector General of a violation of any law, rule, or regulation, or mismanagement, a gross waste of funds, an abuse of authority, or a substantial and specific danger to public health or safety, or (4) any other whistleblower protection.

The definitions, requirements, obligations, rights, sanctions, and liabilities created by controlling Executive orders and statutory provisions are incorporated into this agreement and are controlling.'.''

(2) Agency Websites.—Agencies making use of any non-disclosure policy, form, or agreement shall also post the statement required under section 2302(b)(13) of title 5, United States Code (as added by this Act) on the agency website, accompanied by the specific list of controlling Executive orders and statutory provisions.

(3) Nondisclosure Policy, Form, Or Agreement In Effect Before The Effective Date.—With respect to a non-disclosure policy, form, or agreement that was in effect before the effective date of this Act, but that does not contain the statement required under section 2302(b)(13) of title 5, United States Code (as added by this Act) for implementation or enforcement—

(A) it shall not be a prohibited personnel practice to enforce that policy, form, or agreement with regard to a current employee if the agency gives such employee notice of the statement; and

(B) it shall not be a prohibited personnel practice to enforce that policy, form, or agreement after the effective date of this Act with regard to a former employee if the agency complies with paragraph (2) of this subsection.

(c) Retaliatory Investigations.—

(1) Agency Investigation.—Section 1214 of title 5, United States Code, is amended by adding at the end the following:

''(h) Any corrective action ordered under this section to correct a prohibited personnel practice may include fees, costs, or damages reasonably incurred due to an agency investigation of the employee, if such investigation was commenced, expanded, or extended in retaliation for the disclosure or protected activity that formed the basis of the corrective action.''.

(2) Damages.—Section 1221(g) of title 5, United States Code, is amended by adding at the end the following:

''(4) Any corrective action ordered under this section to correct a prohibited personnel practice may include fees, costs, or damages reasonably incurred due to an agency investigation of the employee, if such investigation was commenced, expanded, or extended in retaliation for the disclosure or protected activity that formed the basis of the corrective action.''.

Sec. 105. Exclusion of Agencies by the President

Section 2302(a)(2)(C) of title 5, United States Code, is amended by striking clause (ii) and inserting the following:

''(ii)(I) the Federal Bureau of Investigation, the Central Intelligence Agency, the Defense Intelligence Agency, the National Geospatial-Intelligence Agency, the National Security Agency, the Office of the Director of National Intelligence, and the National Reconnais- sance Office; and

''(II) as determined by the President, any Executive agency or unit thereof the principal function of which is the conduct of foreign intelligence or counterintel- ligence activities, provided that the determination be made prior to a personnel action; or''.

Sec. 106. Disciplinary Action

Section 1215(a)(3) of title 5, United States Code, is amended to read as follows:

''(3)(A) A final order of the Board may impose—

''(i) disciplinary action consisting of removal, reduction ingrade, debarment from Federal employment for a period not to exceed 5 years, suspension, or reprimand;

''(ii) an assessment of a civil penalty not to exceed $1,000;

or

''(iii) any combination of disciplinary actions described under clause (i) and an assessment described under clause (ii).

''(B) In any case brought under paragraph (1) in which the Board finds that an employee has committed a prohibited personnel practice under section 2302(b)(8), or 2302(b)(9) (A)(i), (B), (C), or

(D), the Board may impose disciplinary action if the Board finds that the activity protected under section 2302(b)(8), or 2302(b)(9)

(A)(i), (B), (C), or (D) was a significant motivating factor, even if other factors also motivated the decision, for the employee's decision to take, fail to take, or threaten to take or fail to take a personnel action, unless that employee demonstrates, by a prepon- derance of the evidence, that the employee would have taken, failed to take, or threatened to take or fail to take the same personnel action, in the absence of such protected activity.''.

Sec. 107. Remedies

(a) Attorney Fees.—Section 1204(m)(1) of title 5, United States Code, is amended by striking ''agency involved'' and inserting ''agency where the prevailing party was employed or had applied for employment at the time of the events giving rise to the case''.

(b) Damages.—Sections 1214(g)(2) and 1221(g)(1)(A)(ii) of title 5, United States Code, are amended by striking all after ''travel expenses,'' and inserting ''any other reasonable and foreseeable consequential damages, and]compensatory damages (including interest, reasonable expert witness fees, and costs).'' each place it appears.

Sec. 108. Judicial Review

(a) In General.—Section 7703(b) of title 5, United States Code, is amended by striking the matter preceding paragraph (2) and inserting the following:

''(b)(1)(A) Except as provided in subparagraph (B) and para- graph (2) of this subsection, a petition to review a final order or final decision of the Board shall be filed in the United States Court of Appeals for the Federal Circuit. Notwithstanding any other provision of law, any petition for review shall be filed within 60 days after the Board issues notice of the final order or decision of the Board.

''(B) During the 2-year period beginning on the effective date of the Whistleblower Protection Enhancement Act of 2012, a petition to review a final order or final decision of the Board that raises no challenge to the Board's disposition of allegations of a prohibited personnel practice described in section 2302(b) other than practices described in section 2302(b)(8), or 2302(b)(9) (A)(i), (B), (C), or (D) shall be filed in the United States Court of Appeals for the Federal Circuit or any court of appeals of competent jurisdiction. Notwithstanding any other provision of law, any petition for review shall be filed within 60 days after the Board issues notice of the final order or decision of the Board.''.

(b) Review Obtained by Office of Personnel Manage- Ment.—Section 7703(d) of title 5, United States Code, is amended to read as follows:

''(d)(1) Except as provided under paragraph (2), this paragraph shall apply to any review obtained by the Director of the Office of Personnel Management. The Director may obtain review of any final order or decision of the Board by filing, within 60 days after the Board issues notice of the final order or decision of the Board, a petition for judicial review in the United States Court of Appeals for the Federal Circuit if the Director determines, in the discretion of the Director, that the Board erred in interpreting a civil service law, rule, or regulation affecting personnel management and that the Board's decision will have a substantial impact on a civil service law, rule, regulation, or policy directive. If the Director did not intervene in a matter before the Board, the Director may not petition for review of a Board decision under this section unless the Director first petitions the Board for a reconsideration of its decision, and such petition is denied. In addition to the named respondent, the Board and all other parties to the proceedings before the Board shall have the right to appear in the proceeding before the Court of Appeals. The granting of the petition for judicial review shall be at the discretion of the Court of Appeals.

''(2) During the 2-year period beginning on the effective date of the Whistleblower Protection Enhancement Act of 2012, this paragraph shall apply to any review obtained by the Director of the Office of Personnel Management that raises no challenge to the Board's disposition of allegations of a prohibited personnel practice described in section 2302(b) other than practices described in section 2302(b)(8), or 2302(b)(9) (A)(i), (B), (C), or (D). The Director may obtain review of any final order or decision of the Board by filing, within 60 days after the Board issues notice of the final order or decision of the Board, a petition for judicial review in the United States Court of Appeals for the Federal Circuit or any court of appeals of competent jurisdiction if the Director determines, in the discretion of the Director, that the Board erred in interpreting a civil service law, rule, or regulation affecting personnel management and that the Board's decision will have a substantial impact on a civil service law, rule, regulation, or policy directive. If the Director did not intervene in a matter before the Board, the Director may not petition for review of a Board decision under this section unless the Director first petitions the Board for a reconsideration of its decision, and such petition is denied. In addition to the named respondent, the Board and all other parties to the proceedings before the Board shall have the right to appear in the proceeding before the court of appeals. The granting of the petition for judicial review shall be at the discretion of the court of appeals.''.

Sec. 109. Prohibited Personnel Practices Affecting the Transportation Security Administration

(a) In General.—Chapter 23 of title 5, United States Code, is amended—

(1) by redesignating sections 2304 and 2305 as sections

2305 and 2306, respectively; and

(2) by inserting after section 2303 the following:

''§ 2304. Prohibited personnel practices affecting the Transportation Security Administration

''(a) In General.—Notwithstanding any other provision of law, any individual holding or applying for a position within the Transportation Security Administration shall be covered by—

''(1) the provisions of section 2302(b) (1), (8), and (9);

''(2) any provision of law implementing section 2302(b)

(1), (8), or (9) by providing any right or remedy available to an employee or applicant for employment in the civil service;

and ''(3) any rule or regulation prescribed under any provision of law referred to in paragraph (1) or (2).

''(b) Rule Of Construction.—Nothing in this section shall be construed to affect any rights, apart from those described in subsection (a), to which an individual described in subsection (a) might otherwise be entitled under law.''

(b) Technical and Conforming Amendment.—The table of sections for chapter 23 of title 5, United States Code, is amended by striking the items relating to sections 2304 and 2305, respec- tively, and inserting the following:

''2304. Prohibited personnel practices affecting the Transportation Security Adminis- tration.

''2305. Responsibility of the Government Accountability Office.

''2306. Coordination with certain other provisions of law.''.

(c) Effective Date.—The amendments made by this section shall take effect on the date of enactment of this section.

Sec. 110. Disclosure of Censorship Related to Research, Analysis, or Technical Information

(a) Definitions.—In this subsection—

(1) the term ''agency'' has the meaning given under section 2302(a)(2)(C) of title 5, United States Code;

(2) the term ''applicant'' means an applicant for a covered position;

(3) the term ''censorship related to research, analysis, or technical information'' means any effort to distort, misrepresent, or suppress research, analysis, or technical information;

(4) the term ''covered position'' has the meaning given under section 2302(a)(2)(B) of title 5, United States Code;

(5) the term ''employee'' means an employee in a covered position in an agency; and

(6) the term ''disclosure'' has the meaning given under section 2302(a)(2)(D) of title 5, United States Code.

(b) Protected Disclosure.—

(1) In General.—Any disclosure of information by an employee or applicant for employment that the employee or applicant reasonably believes is evidence of censorship related to research, analysis, or technical information—

(A) shall come within the protections of section 2302(b)(8)(A) of title 5, United States Code, if—

(i) the employee or applicant reasonably believes that the censorship related to research, analysis, or technical information is or will cause—

(I) any violation of law, rule, or regulation;

or

(II) gross mismanagement, a gross waste of funds, an abuse of authority, or a substantial and specific danger to public health or safety; and

(ii) such disclosure is not specifically prohibited by law or such information is not specifically required by Executive order to be kept classified in the interest of national defense or the conduct of foreign affairs; and

(B) shall come within the protections of section 2302(b)(8)(B) of title 5, United States Code, if—

(i) the employee or applicant reasonably believes that the censorship related to research, analysis, or technical information is or will cause—

(I) any violation of law, rule, or regulation;

or

(II) gross mismanagement, a gross waste of funds, an abuse of authority, or a substantial and specific danger to public health or safety; and

(ii) the disclosure is made to the Special Counsel, or to the Inspector General of an agency or another person designated by the head of the agency to receive such disclosures, consistent with the protection of sources and methods.

(2) Disclosures Not Excluded.—A disclosure shall not be excluded from paragraph (1) for any reason described under section 2302(f)(1) or (2) of title 5, United States Code.

(3) Rule of Construction.—Nothing in this section shall be construed to imply any limitation on the protections of employees and applicants afforded by any other provision of law, including protections with respect to any disclosure of information believed to be evidence of censorship related to research, analysis, or technical information.

Sec. 111. Clarification of Whistleblower Rights for Critical Infrastructure Information

Section 214(c) of the Homeland Security Act of 2002 (6 U.S.C. 133(c)) is amended by adding at the end the following: ''For purposes of this section a permissible use of independently obtained information includes the disclosure of such information under section 2302(b)(8) of title 5, United States Code.''.

Sec. 112. Advising Employees Of Rights

Section 2302(c) of title 5, United States Code, is amended by inserting '', including how to make a lawful disclosure of informa- tion that is specifically required by law or Executive order to be kept classified in the interest of national defense or the conduct of foreign affairs to the Special Counsel, the Inspector General of an agency, Congress, or other agency employee designated to receive such disclosures'' after ''chapter 12 of this title''.

Sec. 113. Special Counsel Amicus Curiae Appearance

Section 1212 of title 5, United States Code, is amended by adding at the end the following:

''(h)(1) The Special Counsel is authorized to appear as amicus curiae in any action brought in a court of the United States related to section 2302(b) (8) or (9), or as otherwise authorized by law. In any such action, the Special Counsel is authorized to present the views of the Special Counsel with respect to compliance with section 2302(b) (8) or (9) and the impact court decisions would have on the enforcement of such provisions of law.

''(2) A court of the United States shall grant the application of the Special Counsel to appear in any such action for the purposes described under subsection (a).''.

Sec. 114. Scope of Due Process

(a) SPECIAL COUNSEL.—Section 1214(b)(4)(B)(ii) of title 5, United States Code, is amended by inserting '', after a finding that a protected disclosure was a contributing factor,'' after ''ordered if''

(b) Individual Action.—Section 1221(e)(2) of title 5, United States Code, is amended by inserting '', after a finding that a protected disclosure was a contributing factor,'' after ''ordered if''.

Sec. 115. Nondisclosure Policies, Forms, and Agreements

(1) Requirement.—Each agreement in Standard Forms 312 and 4414 of the Government and any other nondisclosure policy, form, or agreement of the Government shall contain the following statement: ''These provisions are consistent with and do not supersede, conflict with, or otherwise alter the employee obligations, rights, or liabilities created by existing statute or Executive order relating to (1) classified information, (2) communications to Congress, (3) the reporting to an Inspector General of a violation of any law, rule, or regulation, or mismanagement, a gross waste of funds, an abuse of authority, or a substantial and specific danger to public health or safety, or (4) any other whistleblower protection. The definitions, requirements, obligations, rights, sanctions, and liabilities created by controlling Executive

orders and statutory provisions are incorporated into this agreement and are controlling.''.

(2) Agency Websites.—Agencies making use of any non-disclosure policy, form, or agreement shall also post the statement required under paragraph (1) on the agency website, accompanied by the specific list of controlling Executive orders and statutory provisions.

(3) Enforceability.—

(A) In General.—Any nondisclosure policy, form, or agreement described under paragraph (1) that does not contain the statement required under paragraph (1) may not be implemented or enforced to the extent such policy, form, or agreement is inconsistent with that statement.

(B) Nondisclosure Policy, Form, or Agreement In EFFECT BEFORE THE EFFECTIVE DATE.—With respect to a nondisclosure policy, form, or agreement that was in effect before the effective date of this Act, but that does not contain the statement required under paragraph (1) for implementation or enforcement—

(i) it shall not be a prohibited personnel practice to enforce that policy, form, or agreement with regard to a current employee if the agency gives such employee notice of the statement; and

(ii) it shall not be a prohibited personnel practice to enforce that policy, form, or agreement after the effective date of this Act with regard to a former employee if the agency complies with paragraph (2).

(b) Persons Other Than Government Employees.—Notwithstanding subsection (a), a nondisclosure policy, form, or agreement that is to be executed by a person connected with the conduct of an intelligence or intelligence-related activity, other than an employee or officer of the United States Government, may contain provisions appropriate to the particular activity for which such document is to be used. Such policy, form, or agreement shall, at a minimum, require that the person will not disclose any classified information received in the course of such activity unless specifically authorized to do so by the United States Government.

Such nondisclosure policy, form, or agreement shall also make it clear that such forms do not bar disclosures to Congress or to an authorized official of an executive agency or the Department of Justice that are essential to reporting a substantial violation of law, consistent with the protection of sources and methods.

Sec. 116. Reporting Requirements

(a) Government Accountability Office.—

(1) Report.—Not later than 4 years after the date of enactment of this Act, the Comptroller General shall submit a report to the Committee on Homeland Security and Governmental Affairs of the Senate and the Committee on Oversight and Government Reform of the House of Representatives on the implementation of this title.

(2) Contents.—The report under this subsection shall include—

(A) an analysis of any changes in the number of cases filed with the Merit Systems Protection Board alleging violations of section 2302(b)(8) or (9) of title 5, United States Code, since the effective date of this Act;

(B) the outcome of the cases described under subparagraph (A), including whether or not the Merit Systems Protection Board, the United States Court of Appeals for the Federal Circuit, or any other court determined the allegations to be frivolous or maliciou s as well as a recommendation whether Congress should grant the Merit Systems Protection Board summary judgment authority for cases described under subparagraph (A);

(C) a recommendation regarding whether Congress should grant jurisdiction for some subset of cases described under subparagraph (A) to be decided by a district court of the United States and an evaluation of the impact that would have on the Merit Systems Protection Board and the Federal court system; and

(D) any other matter as determined by the Comptroller General.

(b) Merit Systems Protection Board.—

(1) In General.—Each report submitted annually by the Merit Systems Protection Board under section 1116 of title 31, United States Code, shall, with respect to the period covered by such report, include as an addendum the following:

(A) Information relating to the outcome of cases decided by the Merit Systems Protection Board during the period covered by such report in which violations of section 2302(b)(8) or (9)(A)(i), (B)(i), (C), or (D) of title 5, United States Code, were alleged.

(B) The number of such cases filed in the regional and field offices, and the number of petitions for review filed in such cases, during the period covered by such report, and the outcomes of any such cases or petitions for review (irrespective of when filed) decided during such period.

(2) First Report.—The first report described under paragraph (1) submitted after the date of enactment of this Act shall include an addendum required under that paragraph that covers the period beginning on the

effective date of this Act and ending at the end of the fiscal year in which such effective date occurs.

Sec. 117. Whistleblower Protection Ombudsman

(a) In General.—Section 3 of the Inspector General Act of 1978 (5 U.S.C. App.) is amended by striking subsection (d) and ‘‘(d)(1) Each Inspector General shall, in accordance with applicable laws and regulations governing the civil service—

‘‘(A) appoint an Assistant Inspector General for Auditing who shall have the responsibility for supervising the perform- ance of auditing activities relating to programs and operations of the establishment;

‘‘(B) appoint an Assistant Inspector General for Investiga- tions who shall have the responsibility for supervising the performance of investigative activities relating to such pro- grams and operations; and

‘‘(C) designate a Whistleblower Protection Ombudsman who shall educate agency employees—

‘‘(i) about prohibitions on retaliation for protected disclosures; and

‘‘(ii) who have made or are contemplating making a protected disclosure about the rights and remedies against retaliation for protected disclosures.

‘‘(2) The Whistleblower Protection Ombudsman shall not act as a legal representative, agent, or advocate of the employee or former employee.

‘‘(3) For the purposes of this section, the requirement of the designation of a Whistleblower Protection Ombudsman under para- graph (1)(C) shall not apply to—

‘‘(A) any agency that is an element of the intelligence community (as defined in section 3(4) of the National Security Act of 1947 (50 U.S.C. 401a(4))); or

‘‘(B) as determined by the President, any executive agency or unit thereof the principal function of which is the conduct of foreign intelligence or counter intelligence activities.’’.

(b) Technical and Conforming Amendment.—Section 8D(j) of the Inspector General Act of 1978 (5 U.S.C. App.) is amended— (1) by striking ‘‘section 3(d)(1)’’ and inserting ‘‘section

3(d)(1)(A)’’; and

(2) by striking ‘‘section 3(d)(2)’’ and inserting ‘‘section

3(d)(1)(B)’’.

(c) SUNSET.—

(1) IN GENERAL.—The amendments made by this section shall cease to have effect on the date that is 5 years after the date of enactment of this Act.

(2) Return To Prior Authority.—Upon the date described in paragraph (1), section 3(d) and section 8D(j) of the Inspector General Act of 1978 (5 U.S.C. App.) shall read as such sections read on the day before the date of enactment of this Act.

Title II—Savings Clause; Effective Date

SEC. 201. Savings Clause.

Nothing in this Act shall be construed to imply any limitation on any protections afforded by any other provision of law to employees and applicants

SEC. 202. Effective Date.

Except as otherwise provided in section 109, this Act shall take effect 30 days after the date of enactment of this Act.

Approved November 27, 2012.

INDEX

T

U

V

W